Shudders aplenty here, poetically nuanced...ranges across the supernatural spectrum with the fervor of Poe and the aloofness of Lovecraft.— Paul DiFilippo, *Asimov's SF Magazine*

Rutherford is first and foremost a storyteller. He writes poetry for an audience, one that he feels would come back to poetry if only there were poetry to come back to.— *Radio Void*

Fantastic, rebellious poetry!— *FactSheet 5*

Real poetry! Wonderful!— Ray Bradbury

The Rutherford poetry is a delight. I am in complete agreement with his comments on the state of poetry in America today, and pleased that he has chosen to go against the current. His work is his most eloquent argument.—Robert Bloch, author of *Psycho* and *Yours Truly, Jack the Ripper*

Equal parts Poe, Shelley, Lovecraft and Bradbury ...composed with a firm sense of poetics and orchestrated with a respect for poetic tradition....Though written in free verse, they scan with a rhythmic coherence, a dividend of precise word choices and the embedding of alliterative phrases in the line.—Stefan Dziemianowicz, *Crypt of Cthulhu*

This prolific poet who celebrates H.P. Lovecraft and Poe has reached an assurance of craft and in mood... an extraordinary poet, a neo-romantic perhaps, but also Ovid blended with Virgil.—*Home Planet News*

The High Priest of Providence's ghoulie underground...—*The Nice Paper*

Be afraid. Be very afraid. ... Like Lovecraft, Rutherford integrates terrestrial terrors with a more sublime, or cosmic, dread.— Justin Wolff, *The Providence Phoenix*

Also by BRETT RUTHERFORD

POETRY
Songs of the I and Thou (1968)
City Limits (1970)
The Pumpkined Heart: Pennsylvania Poems (1973, 2012)
Thunderpuss: In Memoriam (1987)
Prometheus on Fifth Avenue (1987)
At Lovecraft's Grave (1988)
In Chill November (1990)
Poems from Providence (1991, 2011)
Twilight of the Dictators (with Pieter Vanderbeck) (1992, 2009)
Knecht Ruprecht, or the Bad Boy's Christmas (1992)
The Gods As They Are, On Their Planets (2005)
Things Seen in Graveyards (2007)
Doctor Jones and Other Terrors (2008)
Anniversarius: The Book of Autumn (1984, 1986, 1996, 2011)
An Expectation of Presences (2012)
Trilobite Love Song (2014)

PLAYS
*Night Gaunts: An Entertainment Based on the Life and Work
of H.P. Lovecraft* (1993, 2005)

NOVELS
Piper (with John Robertson) (1985)
The Lost Children (1988)

AS EDITOR/PUBLISHER
May Eve: A Festival of Supernatural Poems (1975)
*Last Flowers: The Romance Poems of Edgar Allan Poe
and Sarah Helen Whitman* (1987, 2003, 2008, 2011)
M.G. Lewis's *Tales of Wonder.* Annotated edition. (2010, 2012)
A.T. Fitzroy. *Despised and Rejected.* Annotated edition. (2010)
Death and the Downs: The Poetry of Charles Hamilton Sorley.
Annotated edition. (2010)
Tales of Terror: The Supernatural Poem Since 1800 (2014)

WHIPPOORWILL ROAD

A Booke of Vampyres,
Incubi, Demons,
Werewolves & Various
Monsters, Along With
Gods & Madmen,
All Told in Poems
To Delight the Knowing &
Seduce the Innocent.

FIFTH EDITION, EXPANDED

by BRETT
RUTHERFORD

GRIM REAPER BOOKS/
THE POET'S PRESS

Fifth *Edition, Expanded and Revised 2012.*
Thirty-three poems in this book appeared in the first edition;
many have been substantially revised or expanded.

Some of the poems in this book have appeared
in the following magazines:
Starlog, Weird Tales, Stone Soup (Boston), *The Rift, Lovecraft Studies,*
Crypt of Cthulhu, Haunts, Poets Fortnightly, Midnight Graffiti, Beyond,
Boston Sidewalk Stethoscope, Sensations Magazine, East Side Monthly
(Providence), and *The Akashic Record of the Antarctic Astral Convention.*

This is the 200th publication of
THE POET'S PRESS
2209 Murray Ave #3 / Pittsburgh, PA 15217
www.poetspress.org

CONTENTS

Poems marked ★ are new in this edition.
Poems marked † were new in the Fourth Edition

WHIPPOORWILL ROAD

Son of Dracula

WAS THE PALE BOY with spindly arms
    the undernourished bookworm
    dressed in baggy hand-me-downs
    (plaid shirts my father wouldn't wear,
    cut down and sewn by my mother),
old shoes in tatters, squinting all day
    for need of glasses.

At nine, at last, they told me
    I could cross the line
to the adult part of the library
those dusty classic shelves
which no one ever seemed to touch.
I raced down the aisles,
    to G for Goethe and *Faust*
      reached up for *Frankenstein*
      at Shelley, Mary
        (not pausing at Percy Bysshe!)
      then trembled at lower S
        to find my most desired,
        most dreamt-of:
Bram Stoker's *Dracula*.

This was the door to years of dreams,
    and waking dreams of dreams.
I lay there nights,
the air from an open window chilling me,

<11>

waiting for the bat,
    the creeping mist,
            the leaping wolf,
the caped, lean stranger.

Lulled by the lap of curtains, the false
sharp scuttle of scraping leaves,
I knew the night as the dead must know it,
waiting in caskets, dressed
in clothes that no one living could afford to wear.

The river town of blackened steeples,
    vile taverns and shingled miseries
had no appeal to Dracula. Why would he come
when we could offer no castle,
no Carfax Abbey, no teeming streets
from which to pluck a victim?

My life — it seemed so unimportant then —
lay waiting for its sudden terminus,
its sleep and summoning to an Undead
sundown. How grand it would have been
to rise as the adopted son of Dracula!

I saw it all:
how no one would come to my grave
to see my casket covered with loam.
My mother and her new, loutish husband
would drink the day away at the Moose Club;
my brother would sell my books
    to buy new baseball cards;
my teachers' minds slate clean
    forgetting me as they forgot all
    who passed beneath and out their teaching.
No one would hear the summoning
    as my new father called me:
Nosferatu! Arise! Arise! Nosferatu!

<12>

And I would rise,
    slide out of soil
        like a snake from its hollow.
He would touch my torn throat.
The wound would vanish.
He would teach me the art of flight,
the rules of the hunt,
    the secret of survival.

I would not linger
    in this town for long.
One friend, perhaps,
    I'd make into a slave
    to serve my daytime needs
(guarding my coffin,
    disposing of blood-drained bodies) —
as for the rest
of this forsaken hive of humankind,
I wouldn't deign to drink its blood,
    the dregs of Europe

We would move on
    to the cities.
The pale aristocrat and his thin son
   attending the Opera, the Symphony,
   mingling at Charity Balls,
Robin to his Batman,
    cape shadowing cape,
    fang for fang his equal soon
        at choosing whose life
            deserved abbreviation.

A fine house we'd have:
    a private crypt below
        the best marbles
            the finest silk, mahogany, brass
            for the coffin fittings,

<13>

our Undead mansion above
    filled to the brim with books and music...

I waited — waited —
    He never arrived.

My fifteenth year I had a night-long nosebleed,
as though my Undead half had bitten me,
drinking from within. I woke in white
of hospital bed, my veins refreshed
with the hot blood of strangers.

Tombstones gleamed across the hill,
lit up all night in hellish red
from the never-sleeping iron furnaces.
Leaves danced before the wardroom windows,
blew out and up to a vampire moon.
I watched it turn from copper to crimson,
        its bloating fall to treeline,
        its deliberate feeding
    on corpuscles of oak and maple,
        one baleful eye unblinking.

A nurse brought in a tiny radio.
One hour a night of symphony
was all the beauty this city could endure —
I held it close to my ear, heard Berlioz'
Fantastic Symphony: the gallows march,
the artist's Undead resurrection
amid the Witches' Sabbath.

I asked for paper.
The pen leaped forth and suddenly I knew
that I had been transformed.
I was a being of Night, I was Undead
since all around me were Unalive.

<14>

I saw what they could never see,
walked realms of night and solitude
where law and custom crumbled.
I was a poet.
I would feed on Beauty for blood,
  I would make wings of words,
    I would shun the Cross of complacency.
A cape would trail behind me always.

<15>

A Letter to Mummy

Your son, he's so —
    Search me for adjectives, ma mere —
    flexible?
        malleable?
            adaptable?
Yes, I like that: adaptable.
Your boneless breast of
    son was born just so,
    without a solid frame
    to stand me up.

So here I am at my majority,
    a knee-crawler,
    a roller, adept
    at navigation with pseudopods,
a scream at parties,
    creator's clay unbaked,
    man of a thousand
        silly putty faces

Where were you, ma mere,
    while I was doughing up
    from babyhood to boy?
Wish you were here
    those postcards from
    Paris and Marrakech,
    your whims
        your escapes
    from seeing me
But on my streets
    my tree'd
    cruel-bully streets
tormentors could find me easily.

Here comes No-Legs!

<16>

I've been stamped into the ground
tug-of-war taffy pulled
stuck like a wad of gum in crevices
waffled by boots in sewer grates.
And all because of you, ma mere;
    those horn-rimmed therapists
    bone-meal-and-mud-baths
    milk cures and calcium
are only the salve on the guilt that bore me.

You see, I've learned today
    my real inheritance —
what I could be/have been
if you had married my father.

The book before me reads:
    Begotten on mortal maids,
    the Vampire's children
    have no bones

If you had married him,
    I'd be here
        full-boned, and more:
I'd have his wings,
    night flyer
    moon swimmer.

Because you balked
    at drinking his blood
    (the wedding rite)
I cannot slake this
    marrowbone thirst:
    I have no teeth.
My lips upon a woman's neck
    a moth against glass.
Did no one warn you
during your pregnancy?
Or did you, knowing,
persist in your refusals,

<17>

hang garlic on the window sill,
watching his leaden face,
his pleading eyes
until the dawn-pink sky
singed him away?

You cheated him—
    he left your veins half-full,
    your womb inflamed
    to make you his bride

It was a dalliance,
a beauty from Boston/
a dark Rumanian:
his castle, his bed,
his bite, the fantasy,
conceiving me
careless in Bucharest.

<18>

Scenes from A Mexican Vampire Movie

THE VAMPIRE CORNERS HIS NEMESIS.
Federico Van Helsing has lost the crucifix,
the holy water, the sacred Host.
His eyes gleam terror beneath his hat brim.
Dracula has an even bigger sombrero.
Each time he closes in, fangs extended,
their hats collide and rebuff him.
Castanets click on the sound track.

He won't take off the sombrero, of course:
a tiny bald spot on the back of his head,
a matter of pride and machismo.

"Next time, Van Helsing!" he swears,
retreating. "Next time I'll get you!"

2
He flees the bedroom of Doña Lucia
in haste when the rooster crows.
The lady was willing, the duenna
hypnotized. But they spent all night
shifting the statue of the Virgin,
turning the holy paintings to the wall,
unnailing the crucifix over the bed,
removing the Bibles. He counted
a dozen rosaries between them,
paced and smoked a long cigar
as they untangled the jangling beads,
trying to get the lady undressed
and ready. Hungry and pained
by the lambent sunlight he curses
them, bursts into a cloud of mist,
drifts out the open window.
"Wait, oh wait!" cries Doña Lucia,
"I'm almost ready!" Just two more
rosaries to disentangle, just one

<19>

more necklace with the Sacred Heart —
these modern vampires just don't
appreciate foreplay!

3
Things go wrong
at the American border.
The vampire's coffin is opened,
the soil sifted by guards
snooping for cocaine,
for seeds and sprouts of pot.
They rip the casket lining,
for suspected bags of heroin.
They shrug, wipe dirt
from his Transylvanian grave
on their trousers, wave
the hearse through. The coffin
is a shambles. His priceless
soil drifts out, the deadly
rays of sun intrude.
His castle is reduced to
a leaky shanty,
entering California like an Okie.

4
Lucky for him, he flew north,
his bat wings skimming the Rio Grande.
He plans to meet up with his coffin later.
A furtive wetback supplies his dinner,
a slash and suck, fast food al dente.
He meets the hearse at the rendezvous,
listens smiling to the chatter of the driver,
the bug-eater Renfeldez, who drools
describing the L.A. Cockroaches.

<20>

He takes a hammer to repair his coffin,
smooths the layer of native soil,
crawls inside with the worms and spiders,
inhales the rich aroma of humus,
the faraway sunset of Carpathia.

Above them, the Immigration helicopter
follows the hearse northward.
"Just that weirdo with the coffin," the pilot argues,
"We checked him —he's clean."
            "Not him," the other
replies. "The guy in the black poncho,
the big sombrero, the guy he picked up
in the middle of the desert.

"We got it all on the infrared.
Let's go down and nab 'em!"

Renfeldez puts down his tequila,
hears the descending chopper,
awakens the master.
The wide-winged bat flies up
to meet them. Nowhere to run,
no crosses or garlic at a thousand feet,
the pilot and officer are easy prey:

never knew what hit them or how
a bat could change to a wolf,
tearing them to pieces,
lapping hot geysers of blood,
letting the aircraft fly drone
toward the pink horizon.

He settles back into casket
a smile on his blood-caked lips.
He likes these Americans,
the taste of cattle in their veins,
the malt of beer, the well-fed
plumpness of their bodies.

<21>

He sleeps to the croon of Renfeldez,
warm in his poncho,
eager for the hot nights of L.A.,
the cool fogs of San Francisco —
over the lid of the coffin,
concealing the Dracula crest,
his bloodstained black sombrero.

<22>

The Spiders

Nature is not all birds and squirrels.
Under your feet cruel orders thrive.
Things you cannot dream of
  or should not dream of
  feed one upon another;
    things feed upon *them*,
every predator a prey,
each parasite sucked dry
by some relentless nemesis.
Look on your lawn —
eight-legged priests in bloated ease
tend their silken tapestries.
Stalk and web make buttresses,
nectar and dew the sunny glow
of rosette windows,
earth throbs with barely audible
enticements of organ threnodies —
deadly cathedral of arachnid gods!

A robed thing (too many legs
to crucify or kill) intones
  Suffer the insects
  to come unto me!
Watch how the chosen victims struggle,
captured in weed-strung ziggurats,
flyers downed, pedestrians waylaid,
sailors shanghaied and paralyzed.
This silken Karnak laced in dew
that only glimmers in early morn
before the sun erases it —
what do its gleamings really signify?

They feast on every unshorn acre —
they seek to make the earth but one
necropolis of wolf- and garden-spider,
eating a billion souls and wanting more.

<23>

There is never enough food,
nor time enough to make more spiders!
Male spiders go blind in a frenzy of sex.
Black widow brides sport hourglass bellies
to count the narrow intervals of mating.
Their egg sacs swell with the death of the universe.

Barn spider giants bask in the sunlight.
Where any beam drops down
    from the heavens,
Arachne scrambles to lace it over!
Behind the walls, beneath
      the well-swept floorboards
I hear the skitter-skit
of daddy-long-legs,
insane horsemen of hunger's apocalypse!

A million spiders in your uncut lawn!
Eight million legs, two million venom fangs!
How many eyes? Some of them have more than two!
They never sleep! They can live forever!
Their stomachs expand to any size!
They have been at it for a hundred million years!
It is better not to think of them.
They do not want you to.
Their webs are meant to be invisible.
They kill and eat and train their offspring silently.
There are more of them every year.
Tear up this poem and do not think of them!

<24>

Dawn

HE THINKS: if someone could describe this scene,
it would be stark and simple, a blond-haired man
leans forward on a folding chair. The air is chill,
though no breath rises from his nose or mouth.
He is quite still, as nightbird songs beyond
the French windows subside to that hush
that precedes the dawn, the guard change
from nightingale to lark. To him,
the room appears to be empty. Although he feels
cold steel through his tight, black jeans
and the damp tug of the back of his T-shirt
to the seat-back, he cannot see himself.
His clothes are likewise invisible to him.

He can feel the breath in his nostrils, press lips
against the back of his hand to prove he is there.
His vision, sharp as an owl's, sees all
that passes on the lawn and garden,
down to the tiniest roil of mouse and vole,
but he is blind to his own hand before his face.

Anyone entering the room would see him.
He supposedly looks awfully good for his years,
three hundred to the day if his memory serves him.
This English house has endured much: riots and war,
Zeppelin and V-2 attacks, the onslaught of blight
and public housing. His well-paid agents
have kept the house intact, managed his gold
with great discretion, and shielded his name
from prying scholars and historians. A blind wall
of trust funds secure his quotidian (quotinoctian?)
needs and secures the multiple vaults, some linked
to one another by passages no rat could fathom.

<25>

He has been the perfect vampire, discreet
in his comings and goings as a Windsor heir,
and London's finest have never discerned him
as a creature of great need and urgency:
a city envelops and forgets so many deaths.

His very contentment, the ease with which
he goes about his business, is the very cause
of his decision to end it — his life — or whatever
this existence is called — at the three-century mark.
He will let the sunlight do it: he waits for dawn
by the eastern doorway, the old drapes
and their dustwebs pulled to the floor, the lace
of even older curtains torn to tatters, panes
broken to admit the acid beams of daylight.

And after this? He assumes: oblivion.
The vampire life did not come with a manual.
The already undead are all clueless; for all
he knows the universe was just one vast
hunger for blood, the feeding and being fed,
the *summa* as well as the *sine qua non*.

Just one thing has him curious:
It is said that a vampire, on dying,
can see his own reflection then,
and at no other time in his undead
existence. All the more poignant,
that he has assembled all the mirrors
this decrepit house possesses:
two sets of dresser triptychs; a pile
of hand mirrors and shaving glasses
(the vanity of guests and how much fun
to creep up on them as they regard themselves
in all-too-flattering lamplight!);
three full-length wall mirrors leaned
    against chair-backs.

<26>

Mirror upon mirror, until the gaze dizzies
in endless fun house angles,
an infinity of floor tiles, chair legs
    and angled corners, eye-twinkle
of the six-armed candelabra
into constellations of ever-diminishing stars,
a kaleidoscope of everything there is,
but not a glimmer of him.

What will they find, afterwards,
if they track his most careless, audacious
killing to this house at last,
or when they come some day to demolish it?
The dust or whatever it is that he leaves behind
like a spilled hourglass? Or just the empty room
with its puzzlement of mirrors, that wide bed
canopied with cobwebs, whose dark sheets conceal
untold congelations of victims' blood?

They will find the clothes, of course:
a closet full of black suits, black jeans,
black leather jackets, black Calvin Klein
dress shirts and T's, all fitting his mode
of "fashion model gone Goth boy."
Yes, too, there's a black opera cape,
wolf-fur trimmed with red velvet lining,
black shoes in every style since 1780
(strange how they never seem to wear out)
right up to present-day sneakers, all black,
black gloves and a variety of useful luggage,
leather, black. Odd that he can only see them
as they hang in the closet: one slip of hand
into a glove or jacket, one toe inside
a shoe or pantleg, and it vanishes, gone
to his own eyes and to the mirror.

<27>

How strange to be real only to others,
to touch a willing neck or shoulders
yet never see your hand doing it, never to sense
except by touch his nose-end, toe or fingertip.
How long it took to become at ease and graceful,
even — to see a wineglass rise magically
before one's one eyes and come to lips,
and then on top of that to have to feign
drinking, to let a wine-wash cross his palette
then fall discreetly back into the glass: that took
a lot of practice! At least the clothes were simpler
now: no more the Edwardian dandy, he slid
into a T-shirt and pulled on jeans as fast
as any teenager. One merely had to remember
zippers and not be inside-out or backwards.

This could have gone on forever, of course,
but the people have grown less interesting,
more easily fooled, more of them glazed
stupid drunk or reeling from drug to drug,
others were smug oxen, waiting the day
their personal savior delivered them.
Who knew it would come, the night
when he could walk into a Goth bar,
and announce "I am a vampire" and silence
followed. A trio of black-clad women
flashed plastic vampire teeth and smiled,
asked which coven he belonged to.
He discerned two types: the overdressed
in opera garb — though none, from their dull
look had even been to an opera — and the
down-dressed in some kind of torn rags
punctuated with metal grommets. The men
in both groups eyed and dismissed him.
No uniform, no admission, it seemed.

<28>

He lingered a while over a red drink
he didn't even feign to taste, his ears
offended by machine noise attempting
to form itself into music. A young man
in the torn pin-cushion mode came up,
made sure he saw the Old English lettering
on his T-shirt that read, "Vampire Victim."
"You're new," the young man said.
He nods. "You're the real thing, aren't you?"
He nods. "Will you kill me?"
He nods. He's happy to oblige, but bored.

There was something to be said for the struggle.
The hunt, and its danger, and the threat
of discovery had been The Great Game for him.
He liked it best when they resisted. Sometimes
he almost let them win, or even escape
in order to overtake and surprise them later.
There was a moment, always, the pause
when he pulled from a throat in drinking
and looked the victim eye-to-eye, a dark
and terrible secret that nature withholds:

the victim in that moment loves the killer,
admires his superior essence, gives up
his life force in abject adoration.
Every one of them said "Kill me,"
if not in words then in eyes' surrender.

What he could never know, was what they saw:
whatever was in their eyes, was not him.

He takes the boy by the scruff of the neck,
and passing the bar he reaches deftly
for three crystal sherry glasses, cupped
between the fingers of his left hand.

<29>

The club, which billed itself Tartarus,
(the place beneath Hell if one needed explaining),
had, as clubs are wont, an alleyway out back,
trash cans and strident ailanthus trees, dark spots
behind high shrubbery against a chain link fence.

Right hand against the boy's chest, he feels
the terrified and excited heartbeat rise
as neck veins flush to readiness, oh, too easy!
He rends the shirt away, leans down, parts flesh
with his expert incisors, inhales the blood
like a breath of fresh air, takes it in fast,
faster than he has done for years, the breath
fails, the heart falters — no! he pulls back,
pounds at the ribcage to start the heart again —
he would not be cheated — the boy's mouth
is frozen in an *oh!* of horror and *no, I
didn't really want this won't you please stop?*

He doesn't stop — he ends the life that bleeds
beneath him, sucks dry the husk of heat,
life and the great force that animates all things
like a great and overflowing battery.
This ought to be exciting, yet in a moment
he is sated, this death as boring
as a fast-food hamburger. What to do
with the body? With strength he knew
no way to measure he lifts the limp form
and shakes it against the steel grid of fence,
firm, then fast, then faster, till bone and tendon,
flesh and skull and garment all pass on through
like cabbage through a grater,

soft wet fragments falling through, as cloth
slides down, a heap of belt and pants and grommets.
This was not his usual, careful feeding. The mess
would be considerable, the mystery
of how a man passed through chain links
a riddle for the local police station.

<30>

Dogs were coming; he sensed them already,
a feral pack that followed him everywhere
and often helped him in the aftermath.
With luck, they would drag off the bones
and fragments: no matter anyway,
since this would be his last feeding.
Re-entering the Goth club, quite unaware
of whether his T-shirt is dark with heart-blood
he approaches the trio of vampirellas
and puts down, with perfect balance,
three brimful sherry glasses, still warm
with the victim's body heat. "On the house,"
he tells them. "Drink — if you dare."
He smiles his best smile, puts hand to lips
and makes a downward, smearing motion
in hopes they will see blood there.
They stare at him, then at the glasses.
He is at the door; he is out. No one
has said a word or moved to stop him.
He hands a hundred to the bouncer, who nods
an assurance of his forgetting his ever
having been there, turns the corner
as the dogs begin turning into the alleyway.
If he were only one century old tonight
perhaps this would be amusing. The weight
of fresh blood within him slows him
and he window-shops on the long walk home.
No one seems to notice the blood all over him,
or if they do they pretend not to notice
another young man's Gothic fancy.

Now home, he waits for dawn.
The sun seems his most reluctant prey:
it just will not arrive on schedule, the clock
seems to have slowed its ticking, the intervals
between seconds get longer and longer.

<31>

When will it end? Does anyone in London
even have a rooster as harbinger
of the upcoming solar disk? The bats,
the owls, have all retired: is that red line
beyond the oak trees the edge of sunrise?

He turns to face the mirrors. It starts.
His eyes begin at last to see eyes, a face,
dark lips, those fine and perfect teeth,
the line of neck to shoulder, the skin,
as white and soft as ever he was twenty.
He leans to the glass: oh, oh,
so beautiful, so —

By some dark instinct unknown to him
his mouth finds his wrist and pierces it.
He watches himself drink from himself,
the blood flows out and inward,
an Ouroboros circle, feeder
and feeding, self-murdering Narcissus,
frozen, visible in the yellow glory
of the morning sunbeams.

He could do this forever. The sun
is doing nothing so long as he keeps
circling the fresh blood inward, outward.
If he can do to this till sunset
he will survive this burning.
Three hundred years more, at least,
he needs to exhaust his beauty.
He could take hundreds more,
or thousands; he could let
all life on earth flow through him.
It need never end.
The universe wants him in it.
Maybe he is one of the Horsemen
of universal doom and never knew it.

<32>

Sunset is only hours away.
He sways in the ecstasy of his feeding,
the sublime dream of untold victims before him.
Now that he knows the difference
between hunger and desire,
there are lists to make.
He will start with the three vampirellas.
Later, the Goth club bouncer.
Night will be his blood carnival.

<33>

The Turk's Mausoleum

IN MONOCHROME MT. AUBURN
        amid the pallor
    of marble and alabaster,
    ice pond and snow,
        there is one burst of manic color:
        a Turkish rug merchant's
    mausoleum,
    hung with a brilliant
    tapestry,
    sunlit from doorglass
    showroom bright.

His favorite Bokhara?
His last request
to keep it from Omar,
his rival, or Habib,
the brother he hated?

Or a ghoulish invite
to grave robbers?
Once in, the door slams shut,
and like a *djinn*, he rises.
Thieves have to hear
his well-oiled patter,
hours of rug talk,
gossip about the Iranians,
complaints about the
cheap carpets from China
that will be the death of him —

What business here
if you're not a buyer?

<34>

Sacrifice

Before a cenotaph
in civilized Mt. Auburn,
we come upon
a desiccated squirrel,
his eyes a maggot nest,
his mouth
a frozen scream —

someone tore out his heart
and made him an offering
on the monument's steps,
legs extended
    into a blasphemous cross,
his vacant rib cage
crying "Murder!"

<35>

Night Walker

TILL IN HER NIGHTGOWN,
the wiry old woman,
nearly a skeleton in satin,
sleepwalked through lawns,
onto a well-known path
passing her mother's grave,
barefoot between the Civil War cannons,
out the back gate,
then down the slope to the river.

Imagine her walk,
untouched by thorn and burr,
oblivious to gravel,
then over rail and tie
without a splinter,
then gravel again,
then down the steep bank
to the summoning waters!
(Silt, fish, flotsam flow
from Youghigheny to Gulf —
how far might she go?)

Cats she'd once fed
watched from the dark
of rhododendrons,
   but did not go to her.
I saw her, too,
   mute and astonished
as she passed the monument
where I had just recited "Ulalume" —

The cold chill current
did not awaken her,
lifted her up from her wading.
Weeds and crayfish
merged with her streaming hair.

<36>

She sank, her gown
a luminescent ribbon,
pulsing like a jellyfish,
for an instant ageless,
Ophelia or water nymph,
Rhine Maiden, Lorelei,
sparked like an electric eel,
and then the water
was black on black.
Her life dissolved
in unseen bubbles.

Who beckoned her?
What star deluded her?
What long-dead lover
    called from the mud
    of the river bottom?

<37>

Night Shift

At two in the morning
three men pry the door off
of a well-kept mausoleum.
Their pickup truck,
concealed in moon-shadow,
idles. I smell, from my hiding place,
    the acrid exhaust,
yew scent invaded by tailpipe vapors.
    They grunt
as a crowbar twists
the iron of a rusted lock.
One man advances
into the dead space,
stands with head bowed
as though in prayer,
    or hesitation.

The moon's full beams
illumine the chamber,
the urn, the wall plaques,
    a wreath
of shriveled camellias.
He waves the others in.
They shake their heads,
    don't want to do
whatever it is they are doing.
He puts his hands
    on their shoulders,
reminds them
of whatever it was
they promised.

<38>

He draws them in.
Together, they push aside
a stone sarcophagus lid.
They make a sickened groan,
spit epithets
in a language I do not
recognize.

They lift, drag something heavy
along the floor,
lift into pickup,
cover with tarp.

One man bends over,
heaves gobbets of puke
at the road's edge.
The other just laughs,
moves to the yew shrubs,
to relieve himself.
He trembles, though,
    as he sprays the leaves.
Inches away, I hold my breath.
He staggers back, oblivious.

The truck pulls forward,
headlights doused.
The three men,
packed tight in the truck cab,
share a whisky bottle,
light one another's cigarettes,
wipe their hands on their
red plaid hunting jackets.
They watch for a long time,
wait for an interval
when no headlight is visible
anywhere, then race
for the gate and the streets beyond.

<39>

The door is left open,
  the crypt a shambles:
the open hole, wood fragments,
what might be someone's blood,
the broken lock.
I read the woman's name,
  Hungarian, I think,
  and her chronology —
  oh, a ripe one! —
   ten years dead,
ten years to the day.

<40>

Trysting Place

I N AUGUST HEAT
the fraternity boy
slips out of his shorts,
slides to the warmth
of his eager girlfriend.
They lay on a pioneer grave,
beach towel on a flat shale-stone,
the lap of lake water
matching their rhythms.

Between the rising and falling
as he stops
to tease her wanting,
he reads the stones,
lit up as headlines
by the leering moon,
whispers inscriptions like names
of other women, better lovers:
  Jeanette...Sarah...Abigail.

The carpet of grass
seems to undulate.
The lake pulls back its waves,
the sky careens
above the maples.
He feels a host of faces
crowd inside him,
their compound anima
a cauldron of passions.

A diaphanous spinster
clicks tongue
against skull-teeth.

<41>

An ectoplasmic virgin
    blushes,
averts her empty
    eye sockets,
yet peeks through
double-skeleton finger fence.
A headless bosom
    envelops him.
Another's tree-root hunger,
roiling amid worms and centipedes,
rakes prickle-nails across his back,
    says *Love me! — Not her! — Me!*
He stands — he screams —
his seed arcs out,
    a liquid aurora,
    dappling the grass
    in its fall.

"Someone — people —
    lots of them — watching!"
    he tells her.

Half-dressed, half trailing
jean shorts and underwear, they run
from the peeping ghosts,
the knowing grass,
the listening night.

<42>

Midsummer Night

I am well-met by moonlight:
Bats line the graveyard trees,
   hanging from pine and maple boughs.
   Not hundreds of bats,
      but thousands —

Their slant inverted eyes regard me.
In their world I'm the strange one,
   a two-leg walker
    stuck to the ground,
dim-sighted, inarticulate,
deaf to their ultrasonic Sanskrit.

I love their wingbeats, their
startled flight when I clap my hands —
their comradeship for my monologues,
their brotherly listening —

And though they darken the trees
so the beacon moon,
the stars cannot intrude,

fireflies assemble
like landing lights,
my faerie pathway clearly marked

into the grove and the elder gravestones,
out to the lake and the quiet streets,
or — to nowhere
I can remain as their midsummer king,
a willing captive of Mab or Oberon,
regent of their passing luminance,
crowned in an aureole of foxfire

<43>

for this night of nights,
    summer's briefest,
its joys paced frenzied, feverish,
from long-drawn dusk till teasing dawn
when batwings fold invisible
into the foliage and the ill-met
day people rise from their beds,
cock-crow and assume their power.

Keep me now and forever,
    thou sable Night!

<44>

West Point

At West Point Cemetery
I come upon the grave,
the mass grave of cadets
who went half-trained
to a Mexican slaughter.
They lie in their shrouds,
   their dress blues,
   buttons polished,
   shoes immaculate;
laid gently like babes
   in a playpen,
side by side in a chaste
   embrace,
stacked up like logs
   for a burning,
smothered with loam and tears.

This ground is covered
   with yellow wood sorrel
the clover-like leaves for Luck
the frail blond flowers for Beauty
the persistent roots for Strength

I tear a stalk and taste
   its lemon flavor,
chewing it slowly —
not some pasty communion wafer
but a Host sublimed of flesh,
of hair and bone and marrow;
not some dark wine fermented
by yeast in Original Sin,
but dew and rain and root-sap
drunk from the lips of the grave.

<45>

Judge Hathorne's Grave, At Salem

A T SALEM
the burying ground
is a garden of stones,
an orchard of oaks.
Acorns burst to grow,
tombstones erase
their shallow tattoos,
becoming anonymous —
Death's heads
and angel wings,
bad poems
consumed by moss,
the promise of Heaven
like Confederate money.

Still there is some
justice — an oak trunk
engulfs the stone
of a solemn Puritan,
roots clinging like
rabid dogs.

He doomed the innocent
as witches and wizards,
to infamy and hanging,
to a farmyard burial
in family shame.

Imagine this —
his grave invaded
by inexorable roots,
the frail box split,
his gradual awakening
as vampire tendrils
invade his ears,
his mouth, his nostrils,

<46>

the circling of taproot
to snap his neck,
his arms and legs
broken and useless.

Doomed to immortal
consciousness
(the Life Eternal!),
nerves and ganglia
a web of pain receptors/

An old woman
condemned him to this.
She spoke the words
on a Candlemas midnight,
took from the hanging tree
where her mother's mother
died innocent,
the patient acorn of revenge.

She wrote his name on it,
pushed it with thumb
into the loam of his grave,

traced runes in blood
upon his stone,
danced the wild dance
of his resurrection —

sang things that the wizened
old ladies of Salem never knew

as there were no witches
in Salem
then.

<47>

The Forgotten Gravestone

At Swan Point:
a level stone is engulfed
by soil and grass.
It settled, perhaps,
or a careless groundsman
neglected it.

Most of the name is gone,
and half the date.
Earth closes around it
like a healing wound.
There must be no family left,
no friends to make worried
inquiries at the cemetery office.

Perhaps he lived abroad,
fought an unpopular war,
was disinherited,
suffered excommunication,
the village homosexual,
married a foreigner,
died in a prison,
drooling lobotomized
in a madhouse,
morphined in an alley

or perhaps, he was a poet.

<48>

The Swan Point Ghoul

Two months have passed
since I stood here,
in magic circle at the Old Gent's
grave, honoring Lovecraft.
The place I chose to stand on —
an older plot by a pine tree —
has dropped by a foot or more,
its earth a moil of root-turn,
brown against green
of surrounding sod.

Did the coffin collapse,
  or was it removed
    by something
    that tunnels
beneath the gravebeds? —

some necrophagic mole-man,
sharp claws on spatulate fingers,
red eyes sheathed in reptile layerings,
teeth jagged and piercing,
its sense of smell infallible,
burrowing from vault to tomb,
to late night lap of pond water,
to daylong sleep in a bat cave.

Even as we stood here,
  speaking our words of praise,
  reading our innocent poems,
did March earth muffle
  the splinter of casket
  the tear of cloth,
the insistent feeding
of the Swan Point ghoul?

<49>

Ɖart Island

ERRY CUTS FOG
   in Long Island Sound,
   baleful horn bellowing;
   a midnight run
   unblessed by harbor lights,
  unknown to sleeping millions;
convicts at the rails,
guards behind them,
dour-faced captain at the helm
  a face and a pipe
  and a dead-ahead glare,
an empty gaze that asks no questions,
  offers no advice

A careful mooring,
  cables thicker than hanging noose
  bind ship to pier;
pilings like pagan columns
  bind pier to Hart Island

Convicts shuffle to the end of the dock,
  guards behind them with billy clubs,
   hands tensed at holster.
You fellas better behave now,
  the captain mutters,
just do what you're told.
And no funny business, another voice warns,
'cause anything could happen to you here.

The prisoners shiver at moonless expanse
of blackened water,
dead shell of Bronx one way,
bedrooms of Queens the other;
clap their hands,
blow on their fingers
to fight the chill.

<50>

Guess you would freeze, one speculates,
before you could swim to shore.

Just do what you're told,
the biggest con admonishes.
I been here before. Do what
you're told and then it's over.
Eager to earn
the early release,
willing to dig
and lift and carry,
they turn to the foreman.
He points to the tarp
 that covers the cargo.

They lift the tiny oblong boxes,
 frail as balsa,
  thin pine confining
   the swaddled contents.
What's in these things?
 one asks, taking on three
  stacked to his chin.
Over there, is all the foreman says,
 pointing to mounds
  where a silent back hoe
   stands sentinel.
These be coffins, the older con explains.
 Baby coffins.

They lower the boxes
 into the waiting holes,
  read the tags attached to them:
BABY BOY FRANKLIN
 CARL HERNANDEZ
  UNKNOWN BABY GIRL, HISPANIC.

<51>

The adult coffins are heavier,
   two men at least to carry each one.
They can joke about these:
    Heavy bastard, this Jose.
      Carla here, she musta wasted away.
But no one speaks about the babies.
The convicts' eyes grow angry, then sad.

Later the mounds will be toppled,
   the soil returned to the holes,
     flattened and tamped
       with a cursory blessing
by an ecumenical chaplain.

These are the lonely dead,
   the snuff-out of innocence:

crack babies
   AIDS babies
     babies dead from drive-by bullets
babies abandoned like unwanted kittens
   dumpster children

No wonder this island cries in its sleep.

<52>

After the Storm

DEAD NIGHT.
I tramp the midnight lane
of yews and mausoleums.
The air resounds with muffled cries:
a cat? a wailing ghost?
a child abandoned
to gusts of rain and fatal chill?

I think of Roman fathers
exposing their infants on hilltops —
or, far more likely in this
ignoble time, a furtive birth
dumped from the back of a passing car.

My eye expands into the moonless dark.
I brush against the rain-filled leaves,
push through the hedge
until I find the source:
on a mound where six markers neatly grew
a tree had crashed upon an infant's grave.

Sleep, sorry ghost
from your Indian awakening!
Was it not here the Iroquois
made secret pledges to moon and stars?
Did they not tell of jumbled boneyards
where felling trees brought back the dead —

not whole, but with the jaws and tails
of animals, were-things with fangs
and claws and antlers, hoofed hands
and legs attached at useless angles.
Hence their horror of disturbing bones!

<53>

Something ascends before me, a blur
between the graveyard and the pines:
I see the outspread wings of an owl,
the twisted arc of its talons,
but it regards me with a human face,
a tiny death-head in a feather shroud,
withered and wise and ravenous
for the mother-milk of the skies.

The Argument

"Two decades ago that scribbler Poe" —
Longfellow smiled and took tea,
— "that jingle writer as Emerson dubbed him,
called us but frogs 'round the Common,
likened our poems to croaking.
Well, he's dead, and I'm writing still,
and that's an end to it."
His auditors nodded, some heavy-eyed,
as the old master recited "Evangeline."

One sunny day, quite unintending,
I find the old bard's tomb in Mt. Auburn:
a grassy knoll well fringed with yews,
a stately monument, the letters
L O N G F E L L O W
immense enough for all to read.
But whom should I discover there,
perversely lingering, casting their shadows
upon the stone that weighs the poet's brow?
Whom but a trio of stately Ravens,
borne on their wings from an unknown shore,
rebutting the graybeard poet's boast,
ending the argument — forevermore!

<54>

An Exeter Vampire

HE COMES BACK,
  in the rain, at midnight.
Her pale hand, not a branch,
    taps the glass.
Her thin voice, poor Sarah Tillinghast
 whines and whimpers,
  chimes and summons you
to walk in lightning and will'o wisp
to the hallowed sward of burial ground,
to press your cheek against her limestone,
run your fingers on family name,
to let the rain inundate your hair,
wet your nightclothes to a clammy chill,
set your teeth chattering, your breath a
tiny fog within the larger mist.
You did not see her go before you,
and yet you knew she was coming here.
Soon her dead hand will tap your shoulder.
Averting your eyes, you bare your throat
for her needful feeding, your heat, your
heart's blood erupting in her gullet.
You will smell her decay, feel the worms
as her moldy shroud rubs against you.
Still you will nurse the undead sister,
until her sharp incisors release you
into a sobbing heap of tangled hair,
your heart near stopped, your lungs exploding,
wracked with a chill that crackles the bones.
The rain will wash away the bloodstains.
You will hide your no more virginal
throat like a smiling lover's secret.
Two brothers have already perished —
the night chill, anemia, swift fall
to red and galloping consumption.

<55>

Death took them a week apart, a month
beyond Sarah's first night-time calling.

Honor Tillinghast, your stoic mother,
sits in the log house by the ebbing fire,
heating weak broth and johnny cakes.
One by one she has sewn up your shrouds —
now she assembles yet another.
For her there is no peace on this earth,
nor any rest in the turning grave.

Storm ends, and bird songs predict the sun.
Upstairs, in garret and gable dark,
children stir, weak and tubercular,
coughing and fainting, praying for breath.
One week more, and they all will have died:
the ones that suck by night are stronger
than those they feed on, here where dead things
sing their own epitaphs in moon-dance,
and come back, in the rain, at midnight.

Exeter, Rhode Island's "vampire" case of 1799 ended with the exhumation and
destruction of the corpse of Sarah Tillinghast after four siblings followed her in
death by consumption. They burned Sarah's heart and reburied all the bodies.

<56>

Mrs. Weeden, of Pawtucket

OMEONE EXHUMED
   in dead of night
   heart of Pawtucket,
   blank eyes of empty factories
   the only witnesses,

exhumed Elizabeth Weeden
dead eighty years now —
ripped off the lid
of her sarcophagus,
lifted the coffin
from a trough of water
      (What smells?
         what scraping beneath
            of clawed, albino rats?)

came in a pickup,
   backed over tombstones,
   ripped up the shrubbery
   to get at her—

but nothing went right
   for these amateur ghouls.
The fine box shattered
   like so many matchsticks.
The skull went one way —
   shroud tearing like spiderwebs
   as bones fell everywhere —

not white in the starlight,
   not white in the beams
of their furtive,
   terrified flashlights

<57>

but black,
digits and vertebrae,
   femur and ribcage
dark as the quill
of a graveyard crow —

They fled with nothing.
Next day I stand
with a Pawtucket detective
who asks me what sense
I can make of this.

I'm not sure.
But last night was Lovecraft's birthday.
In his "Reanimator" tale
a man named Ezra Weeden
is the first revived from the dead,
from the "essential salts" in his grave.
Even in sunlight this tomb is hard to read.
It says "E....ZA... WEEDEN."

A shard or two of bone remains,
black on the stubborn green of lawn,
and everywhere, in tatters,
fragments of shroud appall the sun:
the color is rust, and brick,
persistence of blood, unclean,
outlasting worm and tree-root,
a color which, once seen,
can never be forgotten.
I do not want to see its like again.

<58>

The Exhumation of Goethe

Weimar, East Germany, 1970

BY ALL MEANS do this at night, while Weimar
sleeps, while even those whose job it is to watch
the watchers, sleep. In merciful dark,
the third shift silence when the local electric plant
shuts down for the Good of the State,

take a cart — no, not a car, a hand-drawn cart —
dampen its wheels so your journeys to,
    and from, and back
to the foggy graveyard are soundless.

Do not awaken the workers!
Here are the keys to the wrought-iron gates —
    mind you don't rattle them.
The crypt has been purposefully left unlocked.
You need but draw the door.
The cart will just squeeze through
(Engineer Heinrich has measured everything!)

Open the sarcophagus as quietly as possible.
Watch the fingers! Don't leave a mark
    on the hand-carved cover.
Be sure it's Goethe, the one with a "G."
We don't want his crypt-mate Schiller
(too many anti-People tendencies there).

Lift up the whole thing gently.
The bones will want to fly apart.
Only the shroud, and some mummified meat
keep him in the semblance of skeleton.
Just scoop the whole thing up,
and into the cart like a pancake.

<59>

Here's a bag for the skull. Don't muss
those ash-gray laurel leaves.
We plan to coat them in polyester
after we study that Aryan skull
whose brain conceived of Faust,
Egmont and sorrowful Werther.
We're going to wire the bones together,
strip off that nasty flesh,
maybe bleach him a little,
make a respectable mummy.

Who knows, if he looks good enough,
in a relined sarcophagus,
we could put him on display.
Come to *Kulturstadt*!
See Goethe's body!
Even better than Lenin!
(Can we say that?)

We'll pipe in lieder and opera.
Tour guides will be dressed as Gretchen.
Maybe a fun house
with Mephistopheles,
and sausages at Brander's Inn.

Ah! the cart is here! The bones,
    yes, the bones. Unfortunate, the odor.
We can work on that.
The colors, *mein Gott*,
(excuse the expression)
they will not please —
over there, Klaus,
    if you're going to be sick —

<60>

It's such a *little* skeleton —
was he really so short?
The books insisted
he towered over
his contemporaries.
So much for the books.

And the shroud — that color —
not at all what we imagined.
Perhaps the opera house
could make a new one.

What's that you're doing?
Mein Gott, he's come apart!
The project is cancelled.
Poets are just too — flimsy.
Next time let's exhume a general,
or Bismarck, or the Kaiser,
someone with a sword and epaulets.
Armor would be even better,
since it *holds things in*.
The People want giants!

<61>

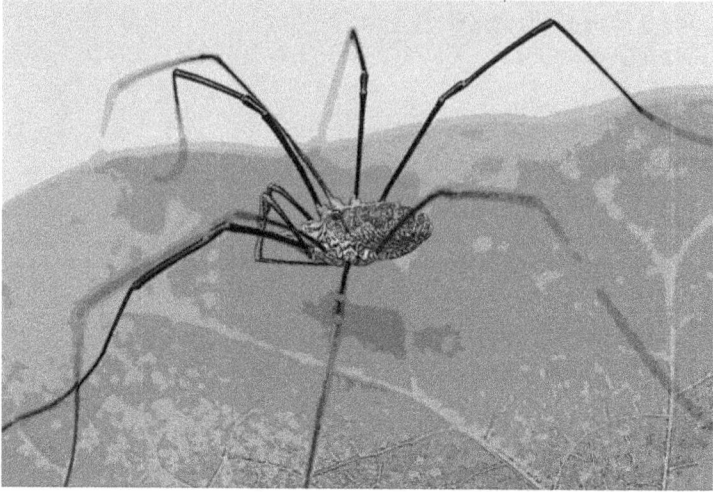

The Harvestman

Day fell. The cooling sun careened and set,
an orange flare behind the broiling hill.
August is full upon the town, and yet
the lakeside grove is desolate and still.

No gravestones bear my surname here —
(my forebears have vanished to scattered dust) —
yet this is where I contemplate a bier,
a monument, a poet's shattered bust.

This burial ground of proud and prudent Scot
is now a blasted place of toppled stones,
storm-blasted trunks and layered, fungal rot,
tree ears and bell-shaped mushrooms white as bones.

The ancient limestone markers, tumble-tossed,
cast off like cards at the end of a game,
speak of loves played and grand illusions lost,
fragmented now to letters from a name,

<62>

scrabbled by giants or angry, spiteful youth,
treefall, or lightning's vengeful, jabbing pen,
first from surname pulled like a broken tooth,
birth date from death, the where of it, the when

now jumbled like a madman's ransom note.
Words carved in stone as certain history
confound the reader now in jumbled quote,
turning church'd facts to puzzled mystery.

Upon an obelisk of limestone, cold
with the chill of glacial remembering,
beneath the wizened shade of maples, old
with a century's Novembering,

a host of Harvestmen ride skitter-skit,
legs tracing Braille of infant's monument.
Daddy-Long-Legs! sly arachnids, unfit
for sunlight, silent raptors, demon-sent —

Why do you writhe and twine those wiry limbs
(too many to count as they crouch and leap)?
Why herd like worshipers entranced by hymns,
then fly like clerks with appointments to keep?

One moment you're here in a skittering tide;
then, as my shadow touches your eyes,
you race to the obelisk's other side,
the way a tree'd squirrel is caught by surprise.

We play out this Harvestman hide-and-seek,
round and round the moss-fringed, ancient grave,
'til I can almost hear these monsters, meek
and voiceless, moving in a song, a wave

<63>

of primal hungering. Bad luck, cursed crops,
they say, if you kill one. Better to dread
their venomless fangs, their sinister drops
from overhanging branch or dusty bed!

What do they eat? What do those tiny eyes
seek out and chase amid marble and slate?
Leaf-litter bugs, dead things of any size,
trapped beneath fangs and feeders (eight!)

Are you the harvesters of suicides?
Do the soul buds of babies appease you?
Do you drink the tears of abandoned brides?
Does the mist from rotting coffins please you?

Your mouths are not for speaking, Harvestmen.
Your secrets, like the truth behind the stones
(how did they really die, and why, and when?)
are told in your thousand-leg dance on bones.

Night now. The knowing moon will rise and set,
an umber globe behind the misty hill.
Pregnant autumn is in the air, and yet
the still-green grove is desolate and still.

All night, ten thousand eyes are watching here,
shepherds tending their ectoplasmic fold,
forty thousand spider tendrils, fear
incarnate, soul vampires, patient and old!

Harvestman, Harvestman, whom do you seek?

<64>

Aceldema, the field of Blood

Why does the wind howl so?
Why, in this holy land
will neither Jew nor Christian
bury their elders here?
Why no flowers ever
in this monochrome graveyard?

This is cursed ground
     where nothing wholesome grows.
Markers and monuments
     are toppled by earthquakes,
     names weathered off by wind-sand,
communal stones from plague times
     (mere icons of contagion),
a potter's field, rock sepulchres,
dry hills honeycombed
with doorless, nameless tombs.

Here slaves and foreigners,
strangers assassinated, whores
     and their discarded fetuses
mingle their bones and dust.

The great old fig trees died —
     a single olive tree
     leans wearily
          against a wall,
its black fruit withered.

Here a millennium of graves
is untouched by robbers —
for even the lowest of thieves
will not seek plunder here.
Whatever is put here
stays here, untouchable.

<65>

ACELDEMA

A. The place of the Cœnaculum.
B. Of the Oke Rogel.
C. Where the Apostles hid themselues.
D. The field of Bloud,

E. The Mountaine of Offence.
F. Part of the valley of Iehosaphat.
G. Part of the valley of Ge-
   hinnom.

The shadows at dusk
skulk by like beggars,
furtive penumbras
en route to better darknesses.
This is a ghostless place
save for the original
owner's spirit.

If you would find a man
    and love him,
as teacher, soul-mate, friend,
and in one night,
    betray him,
so, too, would your soul-poison
envelop the land you purchased —

<66>

the place you gave away
to everyone and no one,
your charity to corpses:
this desolate Aceldema,
deeded for thirty
silver pieces, Judas!

<67>

Miners' Cemetery, Atacama, Chile

Whatever is put in Atacama
stays in Atacama —
a wreath of roses,
every petal intact
in perfect desiccation;
miners' pine markers
untouched by rot or termite,
the wooden chapel's planks
    striated fossils,
unrusted nails a century old,
copper and tin communion cups
    all but untarnished,
the last wine's dregs
a crystal ring.

<68>

The graves are shallow,
the fence a mere
    formality,
for no one comes here —
the miners' mummies
will be miners' mummies
till the sun grows cold.

One thousand miles
of desert coast
surround this graveyard,
the vast Pacific
begrudging one drop
of rainfall,

the only damp
at the cliff-edge
and off-shore islands,
the unceasing splatter
    of guano,
    gulls' gift,
millennial deposits
a hundred yards thick,
the Andes' answer
    to Dover,

<69>

mined by coolies
for explosive nitrates,
then, as luck would have it,
the miners of Bolivia,
Peru and Chile followed
to dig the hard ground
of the desert flats
for the mountains' run-off —
more nitrates, the Titan's ichor,
without which guns
would be mere toys —
nitrates to fertilize
the sugar-beet fields
of pastry-mad Europe —

miners worked dead
in a place
where even their sweat
    was stolen.

Rain comes, on average,
just once in forty years.
If you blink,
    you miss it.
To the dead
    it has the faintest sound,
like the turning of one page.

<70>

MY LIFE AS AN INCUBUS

Water Sprite

WHO MADE YOU,
   this full moon night of lilacs,
   like spring itself aburst,
   made you leap from the bulrushes
      of park lagoon
         bare shoulders wet
from the limpid waters
   your long hair sungold
   bleached white
   in lunary light —

who made your visage
   the sculpted dream
   of surrender
your eyes the blue
   of hyacinth
   of lapus lazuli

who made you run naked
   to greet me
then leap into forest
   of chameleon trees

made your fleeing soundless
   as your bare feet
   sought stealth of moss
as I followed —

<71>

made shards of you dissolve
   in dapple of moonlight
   in fall of blossom
   uncurling fern and
   peeping mushroom —

who made your soft
voice beckon me
leading me deeper in woods
   in circle
coming confounded to a rock
at the other edge of the pool —

made you whisper
as ripples subsided
   from a sinking point:
I am yours: mad angel
   of your destiny.
You will follow me forever.
I will always elude you —
escape to the other surface
   of water
   of mirrors
run through your hands
   like mercury. I am yours. I am not yours.

Who made you? Who makes me
   follow you?

I walk home slowly, inhale
the languor of cherry,
the braggart bloom of magnolia,
the luxury of lilacs —
who could resist this moon,
this dionysian spring?

<72>

It draws us,
   real and unreal
   mortal and mythical
quickens the water to form you,
draws your spirit
   to my substance
my solitude
   to your incompleteness.

Shall I return to find you?
Or shall you seek me out
coalescing from rainstorm,
pressing through windowscreen,
cooling my heat
   with your smooth pale skin,
   the patient ardor of ocean,
the murmur of brooks in my ear,
the taste of dew on your lips,
arms strong as river currents,
the lilac scent of your impossible hair
the clear blue window
of your eyes above me

<73>

My Life As An Incubus

NE IRON-BLACK NIGHT
                of summoning
I found and tried a book of spells
(low Dutch and dreadful Latin
ciphering, peppered with Hebrew,
clotted with phrases in Coptic Greek).
It was rubbish, I muttered —
an alchemist's meatloaf —
the stupefying nonsense of Kabbala —

Yet there he stood — a hoary demon,
now in, now out of surrounding mist.
He wavered, he groaned, his
half-blind eyes avoiding me —
he would not stay unless I spoke,
would not obey
        till seal and sigil bound him.

I read the name
        that charms the Furies,
invoked the tone,
wordless, that gods incarnate
must heed, the chord
that binds eidolons to the chains of matter.

The demon smiled, then.
What would you have, or be? he asked.

I am a thing of books and fancies,
ill-versed in animal passions.
The world of joy has passed me by.
I want —

<74>

Your youth returned? he shrugged.
A simple thing! A lover or two —
A legion of girls or boys
Enslaved to your newfound beauty?

I am no Faust! I answered.
My soul's no petty thing
to trade for a common morsel,
a Gretchen, a bone-dry Helen, no!
I want to be that which no one refuses —
a being of night whom none can resist —
unsought yet irresistible —
the tender lover when love is needed,
the forceful one when force is secretly desired.

An incubus! he marveled.

Incubus/ succubus! I would be both.
Make me the world's nocturnal visitor,
winged, strong and passionate,
invisible and cruel.

Men have sought such companions,
the devil extemporized,
yet none have sought to be
the thing that pleasured them.
I'll give you two to own,
a good diversion
from your moldy books.

Enough of books! They brought me thee,
shape-shifting broker of souls,
gave me the power to ask no end
of favor from the Stygian realm.
Make me a prodigy of wantonness!

Both incubus and succubus?

<75>

Either at will. I want to play
these mammal passions to the hilt.
There lay the coins you must accept
 (The devil scowled at the false tokens).
There are the bounds of Pentagram
I can erase and set you free...

He raised his hand to stop my words.
Enough, enough, my sorcerer:
I see I must serve, and well,
or you will summon me for worse.

Be then, what you will.
I render you unseen, unseeable,
unloved yet irresistible —

He muttered here Plutonian spells
that I half-heard, half-felt
as my prolonging limbs caught fire
and wings splayed out my spine.

Oh, I am beautiful,
enormous, winged and strong!
Now up and out — the night is mine!
So many calls to make:
the list is drawn, and long!

2
Incubus, male god with overarching lust —
Succubus, a female hunger as big as the moon,
I rise yin-yang, contrary mist,
across the silty river, trail steeple tops.
I wing above a Midnight Mass,
mock hushed and kneeling choristers
with Orphic songs of unappeasable desire.
The buzzing litanies pass me by,
scatter like gnats beneath my pinions.
Through walls and windows I hear too well
the human longing held in reserve,

<76>

trapped in music and television monotone.
This psychic babble does not distract me.
I spot the easy prey, hear sighs
from open windows, youths
self-pleasuring, dreams arcing to climax.

I squeeze into a shuttered room. Your room —
you of all on earth I have chosen.
You're reading poetry, your dream
an abstract reverie. The way I want it:
passion where passion is most denied.
I am there; the corner unreached by lamplight
can barely conceal my massive outline,
the silhouette that ought to make you scream.
You drop the book. You nod into slumber.
My talon-fingered shadow extends to you,
until my darkness covers you,
breath matching your breath,
heartbeat in unison, hands cupped in hands.

Amazing! I can undress you with wish forms!
Cloth parts, the buttons explode — you are naked.
My subtle tongue explores you, tastes salt
from the cup of your palm. I follow the pulse
from wrist into brain and I am there

with purple flowers
    mechanical bees,
        a magellanic cloud
            of jasmine and light/

you turn in your sleep, we tumble,
my imperceptible hands guide hips
and legs to a full-length embrace
where/

<77>

festive domes coalesce
    from amethyst,
        the sound of horns
            cracks frozen air,
                a field of quartz
                    gleams gold in sun/

encircling me with arms
you gasp; the tremors that drain
your flesh and your sunburst skull
into me, conclude and quell
into heavy sleep/

I drift off languidly,
gorged with the seed of a race of dreams.

<78>

The Waking Dream

ONIGHT IT COMES TO ME,
    rolls off
the rounded moon that fatted
all week with premonition,
drops in a brownish haze
a frozen thunderclap of thought,
a distillation of drums, a bell
anticipating alarm. It comes!
Telegraphy on bristling hairs —
no need to send a thunderstorm
to tap it out on hills or burn
the message on the trunks of trees —
I hear it! I taste
the spice of ashes on my tongue
before my mouth can say it,
a thought as bitter as cyanide.

Ripe with your fate the earth
bears it like fruit: the rain
that hangs its hair on clouds
withholds the whispered secret —
You woke me from dreaming
into a deeper dream.
Your face appeared
inside my skull
pleading for a neck to fasten to,
your beauty reduced
to fingertips of wind on spine,
dressing itself in rags
of others' memories.

<79>

Long I remembered you,
then fought to forget you.
I walled you away; brick
by brick I lost you,
stopped seeing you
mortared in other faces.
Now, how little I know!
How tall were you, anyway?
How old? What shade was that
within your irises?
What really pleased you?
Your profile is pressed
into my seabed,
yet it is one pale fish
you search me for,
crying out telepathically,
preceding thunderstorm
in rasp of air,
dropping a thread
to anchor us
against awakening —

I open my eyes.
I almost see you.
Yet which is real? You,
semitransparent above me —
or the doused lamp
beyond the bowl of wings?
You, almost perceptible again —
or the hole inside the sun
to which my outer dream
still plummets?

<80>

There is perception
unbearable to know or name —

foreknowledge that fills
the sky with its
concavity, takes root
between my waking
and your invasion.

Have you called to me
because our past
still joins us?

Or does your spirit,
vagrant now,
drift on from bed to bed,
seeking a shelter?

while on your own cold sheets
who broadcasts dreams —
    you,
or the mouthless, earless
socketless Lover
who seizes your breathing —
    Death?

<81>

A Haunting

HERE IS A TIME —
    the unseen interlude
    between the twelve-top
    and the descending one
    (the dark-side moon
  of the clock face)—
in which you await me.
There, painted stars
    upon that vault of heaven
    can neither set
    nor circle the Pole Star.
The trees
    on that horizon
    have turned resplendent gold,
    but no leaves fall
    upon the perfect polygons
    of paving stones.
The moon
    hangs full in copper hues,
    a permanent sphere
    no longer dieting
    in giddy cycles.
The night
    bears warming breezes,
    but no hint of dawn.

You are there
    like the sleeping stones,
    the eternal dead,
    the ever-refilling
    sea —

I cannot join you.
Not for me
    your geologic stillness,
    your celestial patience.

<82>

My clock
   ascends to midnight,
   tumbles to dawn.
I do not count the heartbeat
   between dimensions,
never taste water
   at the cusp of poison,
never permit silence
   to reveal your breathing.

It is enough
   that you are there,
a ghost in my synapses,
   psychokinetic
within the pendulum,
a spring that never relaxes.

You are my bottle imp
of unsought kisses,
a jinn from whom
I make no wishes.
Asleep,
   I am beyond your
   eye-blink affections,
your mercury promises.

Your name
is not the one I call;
your immaterial hand
is not the one I touch;
your form is not
the pressing thing
that pins me to the bed

as I hear the chimes
and count thirteen.

<83>

fête

A thousand stars will blaze and sing tonight.
The livid day has blown before itself
all clouds to leave this sepulchre of sky
    a barren bowl of paranoiac suns.
Come I this eve into my mirthless wood,
this colonnade of grey-striped masts,
to celebrate some lisping, rhymèd love?

<84>

I am Love's Antichrist — my barbed-wire heart
has never beat in time with another's!

Though it is June, I crave the bite of ice.
I send the Leveler, wind fanged by North
to sink its hoarfrost tooth into the world,
crisping the maple red, browning the oak.
I cannot pass tonight where green things hope.
I banish Persephone's corn bounties.
No leaf that has the glint of chlorophyll
can last a moment in my chilling gusts.
Precede me, airborne, wasting Nothingness,
lay for my feet a carpet sere and gray,
a trail of ash from my Hadean robe,
dust of the murdered summers I've renounced.

My eye sees all in inverse images:
the near is far, the far away my toy.
Each chink of sky leaps like a broken pane
from where it hangs suspended on a branch,
or like a painted sliver where the trees
thrust down to meet horizon — it is these stars,
my witnesses, who hover near, while elms,
by web-line weaving architecture thrust
fade to infinity, night's palette mad.

I close my cloak about my throat, hold tight
the leaden box I bear. The curve of earth
blinks out the last scant gleam of the village,
save one blanched clapboard church, desanctified,
which grinds against Pleiades as they rise.
Its steeple breath exhales the lidless bats,
purblind, carnivorous doves of my court.
Fly up and out, and with your leather wings
make me an arbor black with rabid pride!
Along my way, an abandoned boneyard
lifts limestone paws and graven platitudes
against me. I laugh at hallowed places,
defying their passive, limp corruption.

<85>

My eyes spit fire. The unkempt grass explodes.
The crosses singe, the solemn obelisks
crack and shatter, the marble angels fall.
No crucifix or holy sign can stay
what I would call and consummate tonight.

<86>

Do you suspect me? Would even your fortress
of intuition guard against this?
My tentacles of ink reach out for you.
You send a moon, and in its sickly glare
the smoking earth rears up two night monsters —
four horns unfolding red, gigantic,
blood wet and throbbing as they block my way.
Horns become ears, I recognize the heads
of guardian owls, elm-high and screeching
as they snap their beaks, their eyes all-seeing.
I pass in silence through their talon clutch
for they are but conjured — and I am real.

Would you cast dreams against my greater force?
Hurl Elmo's fire against my juggernaut?
Ah, soon, comes my reward for nights denied;
for all the days I circled your dwelling,
outcast while others consumed your beauty;
for those half-loved because some hint of you
haunted an eye or a cheekbone — revenge,
my calm last gift for your squandered passion.

I cough a cloud and let it blot the moon
so that no distant star may hear and mock
the oath that is sworn in the hidden copse.
Here! now even fireflies are dimming out,
now ravens avert their ebony orbs,
now sputter and die, ye will o' the wisp!
Not even a random thought can penetrate
this furry arbor of my wretchedness.

Open the box,
be sure the sacred objects are counted.
Be sure the unspeakable ointments gleam
in the krater-shaped Plutonian cup.
Lay out the black and scarlet vestments now,
set forth another cup with water drawn
blind from a mountain spring in midnight oaths,

<87>

scoop graveyard earth burned free of worms and roots
into the center of the Pentagram,
light the black candle now,
step from the arbor and bid you come:

Hear me, ye formless, boundless nameless ones,
Ye captive essences of fire and air,
by this dread Ring and Stone which all obey
I conjure Ye to take the form I dream.
Give me NOCTURNE, bat-winged and silver-reined
(the beast whom once I saw lust-seeking Pan
ride round the earth in an hour's passing!).

I shall not move, yet on his back my will
shall leap these mountains, beat over cities,
hell-ride the hard Atlantic sea-line,
then swoop, then scan the forest
then fall with unrelenting speed
onto your lawn.

Touch not the door which has been daubed in blood
against my coming and going. Sing out
your piercing call to the shuttered window,
where the cat, whom I have collared a slave
of my impulse, will beckon you to look
at the flat fanged face of my messenger.
In an instant, you are borne away,
your scream to no avail, your bedclothes ripped
as you graze the upper treetops, held firm
in ten claws beneath the throbbing wing beats.
I am waiting for you,
for the sound of descending wings,
waiting for the years denied me
to curl into a wrinkled ball
that some hot maelstrom draws
into its belly.

<88>

I am dancing the death of romance.
Dizzily, you rise from your abduction.
You do not know me yet in this darkness.

I take your hand. You speak my name
in anger and astonishment. Your touch
is just as I imagined it, frail and terrified.
Your eyes would plead your innocence, your lips
would say that none but I have tasted them.
I would believe you for the sake of those eyes,
had I not left humanity behind.

<89>

Your arms invite my dissolution, death
in one touch of your supple shoulders,
but I dare to finish what I started.

Come, love, come stand by me,
let me anoint thy fevered brow,
kneel amid knives and Pentagram,
bowing your head for the severing blow
        or blood's obscene baptism,
and thus, and thus,
with what still trembles in the cup,
with earth, with fire,
with midnight waters I place to your lips,
with ivory rings I now produce
from soulless lead and velvet lairs,

as all the bats take mawkish flight,
as leaves drift down upon your hair,
as stars seal our troth
with burning glaze
I do
thee wed.

<90>

Edgar and Helen

Edgar Allan Poe and Sarah Helen Whitman, 1848

THEY WALK THE SUNLIT AVENUE,
        the parasol
concealing her face as she says,
        "How grand
    you have come all this distance to see me."
    She wears a dress imported from France,
confounds him with a haughty roseate scent.
"I will not permit you, of course,
to fall in love with me."
                        He grips
the black valise. His hands turn white
as sheaves of poems fall out
beneath the feet of Sunday crowds.
"Alas," he says, retrieving them,
searching her eyes as she stoops to help,
"If such were possible, then —
Then it is already too late."

By chance she finds the poem
        inscribed to her
I saw thee once — once only

She reads it and averts her gaze,
pretending to favor a floral display.
The suitor knows he has pleased her.

In the strange rooming house he broods
as unrelenting opiates of memory
draw moonlight *houris* in Helen's form.
He thinks of how he can win her,
sway her will with his eloquence,

<91>

his life and poems at her feet,
merge with her gentle bookish life,
take her back to his humble cottage
or stay in this love-charmed Providence.
He dreams of the thousand ways he will love her.

2
Moon and the flames of candled glass
conceal her features but reflect his tears,
his wild-eyed deafness to her final refusal.
He rages at the insults of Helen's mother —
(how Helen were better dead than married
to a godless drinker of the Plutonian lees) —
chills at the echo of her sister's chatter,
the gossips and slanderers anonymous,
who wrote the warning letters to Helen —
damn them all who would thwart his happiness!

She wears her heavy cloak against the cold,
on top of that a black, superfluous shawl,
as if to italicize her widowhood. She speaks
of the Boston lawyer who loved and wed her,
then promptly died, of how he waits
somewhere beyond to renew their vows.
"For are not souls immortal?" she asks.

Poe says, "Let ghosts attend to ghostly loves —
the living to the living. I love you,
Helen, as I have never loved before.
Our poems speak the truths you would deny."

"Do not torment me with vows of love —"

<92>

"You torment me," he stabs, "with beauty,
with scintillant brilliance of eye and mind,
with promises a suitor cannot mistake,
nor chaste propinquity requite."

He takes her frail, cool hand, cups it in his.
Her profile is cold as Athena, her eyes
turned inward in agony, in thought
of the aged mother, the invalid sister,
the imminence of her uncertain health,
the wisp of wine exhaled
    from the trembling suitor's breath.

There is something more, she says,
than the love of man and woman,
    deeper, darker, born of the flesh
    but asking no boon of the touch.
Poe tells of the chaste love he bore
    for his child-bride Virginia,
how Helen would take her place
    as sister, Muse, beloved.

"Neither by word nor glance, nor yet by deed,"
she answers him, withdrawing her palm
from the heat of his impetuous grasp,
"must you ever show that you love me.
I cannot be torn from my place and time.

We are poets. Our words have loved,
but we are separately doomed to solitude.
We must answer for life when life is gone.
You ask for what I cannot give —
I cannot bear your loving glances."

<93>

Coffined in his sleepless rooms,
he poisons himself with laudanum.
He thinks of the thousand ways he will kill her.
He sees her ravaged on a riverbank,
imprints on her breasts of a legion of rapists.
He sends a gibbering orangutan
to stuff her corpse up the nearest chimney.
He bricks her in with her poetry.
He puts her mother beneath the pendulum
(the more she talks, the faster it falls).

He sets her sister adrift on a raft,
circling the Maelstrom ominously
A raven persists on her window ledge.
The Red Death sweeps down Benefit Street.

At vision's height he dresses and walks
the darkened brick alleys of Providence.
He climbs the steep hill to her corner,
spies the darkened windows above.
He will stand here till dawn,
deceived by the rustle of curtain,
the imagined flickerings of candles,
the creak of floorboards and stairs,
the glint of moonlight on brass.
The clean sunrise will banish him,
burning away his ardent love,
    his ineffectual revenge,
leaving him an empty vessel again,
drifting from this friendless seaport,
south, to court a darker mistress,
a veiled widow who refuses no one,
and whom no one ever leaves.

<94>

Portrait of Dorian Gray

IS HAIR IS BLOND, gets blonder
    with each passing year.
He can discern six hundred
shades within the spectrum.
He knows the names of all the plants
    in England. More than a hundred
works of art are sublimely,
secretly and despairingly about him.
He is more talked about at the Opera
than the reigning diva's high notes.
He has never dieted. Old clothes
from seventy years ago still fit him
perfectly. He is asked for proof of age
on entering taverns and certain clubs.
He has never gone home alone
unless it served to torment
tomorrow's conquest.

Tonight there is a detour.
He is in the old studio in Soho.
He stands before the portrait.
It is the annual visit.
The canvas looms just where
    the Master finished it,
    at just that height
that makes the viewer gasp —
the height of a dais,
    a throne
from which the portrait's eyes
can condescend to gaze —

but he is the only viewer, ever.
The skylight is painted shut,
three locks of unique form
unknown beyond the Caucasus
have never been picked or broken.

<95>

Frontispiece from First Edition of Oscar Wilde's
The Portrait of Dorian Gray, by Henry Keen.

There is only one lamp —
the one he brings,
and whose removal
returns this room
to perpetual darkness.
Its incandescence floods
the coruscated canvas
with the hard light of truth.

<96>

Older, older, older —
new lines, new sags,
new sores and venereal woes,
yellow upon yellow in eye-cast,
worms wriggling beneath
the over-stretched, parched
leather of skeletal breast
showing through tattered shroud —

He nods, and reaches up
as if to touch it, a touch
it disdains receiving.
He notes the scar
below the neck,
a thwarted lover's knife
(dead fifty years now),
around the heart
a jealous rival's bullets,
black tokens peppering
the swollen organ
(What was her name? and his?
They've both been quite forgotten!)

One gouged-out eye,
half-in, half-out
of its socket
still manages
a defiant glint
(that time he lingered
too long at the German border) —
where there were three,
not one grim tooth remains now,
the mouth shapeless, the lips
swollen in fungoid flowering.

<97>

The fingernails are black
and bent as bird-claws —
all in all
a rather appalling thing to see.

But what is this? Upon the face,
instead of its accustomed leer
of vice and lechery,
he seems to think the toothless mask
mocks him, puts on an air
of parched nobility.

"It is my place to gloat, old boy,"
the ever-young Dorian cries,
"not yours!" The good eye
of the painting just glares at him
with a kind of Mona Lisa knowing.

He backs away in nameless dread.
The eye gleams back,
its coal-black iris
encompassing
some kind of ineffable bliss,

as though it had passed beyond
the deferred death
they both would share
for all eternity.

His shaking hands switch off
the lamp; he drags it
a hundred paces to the door,
feels for the knob,
there! back and out,
latch closed, the great
amorphous locks
of adamantine steel secure.

<98>

Enough of that! He needs
the night, the London crowds!
He has his choice
of gallery openings, cafes
and garden parties.
One revel goes on all night.
A place with dark trails
and topiary monsters,
malign in moonlight,
where tipsy guests tip-
    toe to pre-arranged
couplings — one waits
beneath the favored
    weeping beech
with an embrace
he answers carelessly
with an extended kiss,
her tongue in his mouth
as lifeless as a slug.

He wrests away
and leaves her weeping
silently. He keeps
his assignation, too,
in the bamboo grove
with his latest boy
(her brother),
whom he mock-wrestles
into submission.

In after-sighs
the dull boy whispers,
"Ah, couldn't you just die
of happiness?"

<99>

Dorian feels nothing,
or feels, rather,
the dim heat a statue might,
on being worshiped.

In the darkness in Soho,
the portrait suffers a smile —
adds love to its list
of all things a man could die of.

<100>

Lucy, A Verse Mystery

Vacant heart and hand and eye,
Easy live and quiet die.
                    —*Sir Walter Scott*

I.

Providence, Rhode Island, 1848
The bar in Poe's hotel, a proper bar
with deep mahogany paneling, row
upon row of wines to savor, great casks
of low-grade by-the-barrel rum, ales
unheard of except this close to the sea
that brought them — thumb-nosed and snug in the sight
of the disapproving First Baptist Church.
Let Roger Williams frown, the ladies
of the Temperance Society petition:
in vain since the long polished bar was lined
and elbow'd by half of the town's lawyers.
Rank upon rank of tables, niches and corners
sufficed for the lower sorts: workmen
in coveralls to the lean, carousing sailors
ear-ring'd in gold and of uncertain parentage.

<101>

Poe sat with Pabodie, a celebrated local,
a delicate man who had read at law
but had no taste for the practice, a poet
with a melancholy ode or two within him,
but above all a useful man, a man who knew
the nature of men and everyone's business,
a man to sound out about the Power family
whose elder daughter, a widow named Helen,
a poetess, he had come to woo.
An answer discreet affirmed her fortune
a small one, but reliable: property and mortgages,
well-managed by old Baptist lawyers.
Eyes rolled slightly around the bar
as Poe asked about the late Mr. Whitman:
a literary man, to be sure, a lawyer
who defended atheists and defamers
of preachers, a man of calamities
whose winter cold went pleural, and killed him.

And as for Sarah's father, "Ah, the less said,"
was all that Pabodie would offer. "And there's
a sister we don't speak much about." Poe felt
unable to pry more from Pabodie, at least
so long as he remained this sober. Gossip
is best pried with the lubricant of wine.
Poe talked instead of his earlier visit,
the summer of '45, of the moonlight
walk when he had seen Mrs. Whitman,
instantly his "Helen of Helens," behind
the red house in its snug garden, her hand
athwart the single rose she was cutting,
the sudden turn she made, her vanishing
into the cellar door whose soundless closing
stopped his breathing, as though to profane
this vision with any sound were unthinkable.
"I've sent her the poem with my recollection,"
he tells Pabodie, and shows him a copy.
Pabodie reads it and says: "Ah, lovely! A blank verse

<102>

paean to our finest poet. Her eyes — what lines! —
two sweetly scintillant Venuses! She will fall
into your power, rest assured, Mr. Poe."

"There was more to the poem," Poe confided,
"but I ought not frighten this Helen of Helens
with the thought of an apparition I saw,
or thought I saw —"

                             "An *apparition?*"
up went one of Pabodie's black eyebrows.
"You know their garden wall drops down
to the Episcopal churchyard, do you not?"

"I did not note it then."

                             "Tell what you saw,
and I will say if it has some common thread
with what *some* have said about that hillside
and what transpires at night there."

Poe turned over his manuscript, half-read
and half-invented as he spoke memory:
"But stay, pale Prophetess! Hold back the moon
And those hoarded clouds that would conceal it!
Return and calm my frensied observing
Of a glowing form that rises — a form
I thought dead, that sleeps no more — it mounts
To speak its dread name into my hearing.
It spoke — not words in any human tongue! —
Thank God it did not speak *that name* or mine! —
A kind of half-whistled ululation.
Its eyes, two darkly luminous nebulae,
Caught mine, and sparked, and spurned me.
Then, folding in its shroud-like trail, it leaped
With superhuman will to the trellis,
Up, up, vertiginous, three storeys up
And either to roof or into attic

<103>

It vanished: all this in my one heartbeat,
In the darkness of one cloud's-passing."

"What did you make of it?" asked Pabodie.
"You do not strike me, Poe, as a 'ghost' man."

"Ghosts, no! Place emanations, if you will,
or astral doubles our souls send out and just
as easily call back. Call them *wish forms*,
mesmeric force, all manner of ill-will:
there are many things in the universe,
and things we call to a semblance of life
by dreaming them or giving name." He paused.
"I fear the wine speaks now. Perhaps I say
too much and you think me but a madman.
I have made enemies with my science."

Pabodie smiled, and with a deft hand replaced
Poe's empty glass with its brim-full brother.
"What you have spoken of, we know quite well.
There are secrets we keep, and those we tell
because they amuse us and harm no one.
A spectre is haunting St. John's Churchyard.
Ask any of these gentlemen here — ask
and you shall hear the same tale from all."
Here Pabodie elbowed a young lawyer,
ushered him close to Poe for the telling:

"Sir, I could not but overhear. No lies
pass muster in this establishment, where friends
console and drink from sundown to midnight.
St. John's *is* haunted. I'll not be found there
on North Main on a moonless night; I'll not
look down there from Benefit Street above
if there's even a shadow in the place.
Just as you said, she comes in her own shroud,
hangs like a harpy in a spreading beech,
or spreads her tresses on a tabletop grave,
or darts from fence to yew to tombstone.

<104>

A harmless fairy, the sexton tells us
(but rum-full he sleeps, and never sees her).
They say her eyes can catch you, and once caught
you are lured to pass the night there, amid
the worms and moss and broken markers,
and if her eyes catch you, your life is hers
to do with as she pleases Night after night
she'll have you there for her pleasure, your pain.
Point out some wreck of a man in an alley
and all will say: 'Lucy has ruined him.'"

"Lucy?" Poe asked. "Why of all names, Lucy?"

"That's what she calls herself. Sometimes she speaks
her name or a few lines of poetry."

Here Pabodie broke in, "And then she's gone,
as thin as smoke and pale as a firefly."

"So I have seen a spectre — the very same?"

"So, Mr. Poe, it would seem. I counsel you
to keep to yourself your summer vision.
The families on Benefit, you see,
have secrets, and keep them. Monsieur Dupin
would be hard-pressed to decipher them all."

Here Pabodie would say no more, but one
far voice from a distant table called out,
as an old sailor made bid to join them:

"Aye, that's Saucy Lucy y'er speakin o'.
She ain't no spirit, unless that 'spectre' word
is your gentleman's way of sayin' what
we all do see and know too well. Dark nights
she haunts the St. John's graveyard sure enough,
and if she catch your eye, an' it be late
and the sexton be well into slumber,

<105>

then many's the man that'ud go to her.
And as for doin' her biddin', that ain't
supernatural since she be wantin'
pretty much what the sailors be wantin'."

Pabodie paled and, finding a handkerchief,
shielded himself from the sailor's breath.
"I don't give credit to these bawdy tales,"
he said to Poe. "They hear — perhaps they see —
and to cover their fear they *embellish*."

Poe nodded. "For a gentleman, a ghost
suffices, a lonely ghost beyond all hope,
ephemeral, untouchable, some virgin
ripped from her life by contagion."
Poe stopped, choked, put out the glass
for another turn from the wine-cask.

II.
Past-midnight Providence was wide awake.
"The Raven" was requested, recited.
Then arm in arm he walked with Pabodie
to a Chinese laundry's doorway; from there,
having passed a yellow paper beneath it,
and waiting a seeming eternity,
the two poets entered a passageway
far into the hillside, into a damp room,
a ratty, fungoid, wet-walled warren
where a dozen reclining sleepers lay,
and beside them a dozen expiring pipes,
and Poe consented to stay.
When that was done, when dreams
beyond Coleridge, of galaxies borne
on a cosmic wind, of worlds created
from mere thoughts, and as readily destroyed
convinced him of his godhood, and madness —
and that was quite enough of that, he fled.

<106>

Alone as ever, and having walked
Mr. Pabodie to his High Street home,
Poe did what it was Poe's nature to do:
at every moment the most awful thing
he could think of. He stood, at last,
at the foot of St. John's churchyard.
And there were sounds, and with raven hair and
night-dark great-coat he passed for shadow
within shadow as he climbed the hill,
and he saw them, and what they were doing.
And the man fled. And the shrouded spectre
rose up from a cold lime table marker
and her white shroud billowed around her
and parted so she was full upon him
in her nakedness, a *lamia*, her eyes afire —
he felt her will like a maelstrom, insatiable,
unquenchable, to fall into her arms
like the nine-day fall into Hell, or the careen
into an empty grave. Her lips touched hot —
nails raked his neck — and Poe swooned dead away.

<107>

It was dawn when he awakened. In horror
he reached for his clothes about him
and found everything in place. His head
seemed under a great bell, his tongue
as stiff as an iron clapper, the taste
of rust, of iron, in his mouth; he wiped
and found blood there. He looked about
and spied no footprints on the damp earth
save those of his own zigzag ascent.
With Dupin's eye he surveyed all: the street
below, where one slow wagon was passing,
pulled by a somnolent mare; the high street
above the churchyard, seen only in gaps
between the garden walls and houses.
Only the shrubs and trees, and the darkness
of certain nights made this a private place.
His perverse imp had brought him here. And what
of the spectre? Did she hang even now
from some rooftop, or sleep beneath the lid
of a vaulted gravestone? No answers here,
but what was *this*? Poe strode to a gravestone
and found upon it a splendid binding,
a finely-printed edition of a book he knew,
"By the author of the Waverly novels" —
The Bride of Lammermoor. Lucy Ashton
is its doomed heroine: her first love lost,
she kills her bridegroom on her wedding night.
On the end leaf was an inscription, rubbed
out by an angry hand, and "S –A –P."

<108>

III.
"My mother, Mrs. Power." Poe bowed;
perhaps he bowed too deeply, perhaps
the bead-line of nervous moisture
across his brow betrayed him. He smelled,
not Muddy's faint rose, but camphor,
mildew and dampened woolens.
"We are honored to receive you, sir,"
the widow Power said stiffly.
"The honor is mine," Poe smiled, eyes lit
with the importuning son's mother-plea,
and she seemed to soften. He had not slipped.

Now Helen, her scarves aflutter, turned,
as another woman swept down the stairs
and into the dim-lit parlor. His hosts
seem startled. "My sister," spoke Helen,
"Miss Susan Anna Power." Poe bowed
as the slight figure, indifferently coiffed

<109>

and double-layered with a Chinese robe
thrown over a haze of many-layered skirts,
burst between Helen and her mother.
Poe bowed again. But silently, an awkward
suitor's pause on seeing a younger sister,
to outward view, an appropriate
deference to an unmarried woman,
but his inner voice spelled out:
Susan — Anna — Power.

"The Raven has come to roost!" said Susan.
"The Raven comes to seize the dove —" The frowns
of Mrs. Power and Helen's consternation
were what they thought caused her to pause.
But no, she *spied the book* in Poe's left hand
against his charcoal-colored overcoat,
and flying across the parlor to him, as though
in salutation, half-bow, half-curtsey, she seized
the marble-edge volume, nails pressed
into the oak-brown leather with uncommon force.
She spoke in a sepulchral voice, so low
as to seem baritone, and from a distance:

"When the last Laird of Ravenswood
    to Ravenswood shall ride —"
To which Poe declined his head and answered:

"And woo a dead maiden to be his bride."

She parried "He shall stable his steed in the Kelpie's flow."

He ended, "And his name shall be lost for evermoe!"

And deftly, *The Bride of Lammermoor* passed
before the uncomprehending eyes
of the wooed one and the watchful mother.
And deftly, *The Bride of Lammermoor* passed
to *The Succubus of St. John's Churchyard*!

<110>

THE CREEPERS

The Messengers

AD NEWS TRAVELS FAST:
that shuffle of newsprint
along the sidewalk
accompanies no wind.
Disguised as scraps
  these messengers slip by
like tented ghosts,
pale sheets still wet,
    linseed scented
    with printer's ink,
creased into the semblance
of beating wings.
Side-stepping trees,
avoiding hydrants,
they hit the gutter,
file by the wheels
of night-parked cars.
Dogs whine and wince
should they encounter
the solemn cavalcade.

These pages are off
to the newsstands,
to the waiting trucks
at *The Daily News*,
where they insinuate
their black calamities
into the morning edition.

As the trucks roll out,
the early obituary creeps
unseen behind and passes
the marked man.

<111>

The Creepers

for Shirley Powell

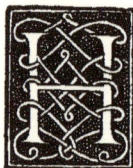

HALLOWEEN:
this is a night for paranoids,
the eve the living and dead
switch places, bonfires of souls
on top of every hilltop,
the night when life
walks tightropes over emptiness,
when autumn finally shrugs
its sorry burden of summer.

This night I am not flesh —
I am a web of ganglia,
a sensitive antenna
to every flow of energy.
I hear the droning wind,
hard-edged as needles.
wearing down stone
a micron at a serving.
I hear clouds scream
as they graze the metal edge
of shining office towers.

On the long cab ride homeward,
above the hiss of tires,
Tenth Avenue lampposts
utter a shrill soprano
of throbbing fluorescence.
Faceless figures shuffle by.
Tenements blur
to corrugated slabs
of half-seen brick,
yet I hear the whirring compressors
of a thousand air conditioners.

<112>

Latin songs bounce
off unlit pavement;
amorphous drumming
fills an empty warehouse.
Stop light: a clutch
of desperate hands
thrusts from a heap of coats
too old and shapeless
to issue more
than an extended palm.

Ticked off in taxi meter dimes,
the pumpkin stroke arrives.
Midnight finds me
on Ninety-Fifth Street, my block
a corridor of feral eyes
gleaming in cellarways
(of all in this raucous city
only the cats know how to be silent!)

The trash can at the curb is rattling,
yard leavings jumbled with broken glass —
hagwig of brittle branch chattering,
a spear of broken mirror
peels off its silver backing
like a witch's unwanted reflection.
Sharp shards are frozen thunderbolts;
their desolate wind chimes clash.
I dare not touch them —
so hungry for a vein to slash!

Over my gloomy lintel
ivy sucks stone and air,
wrinkles with autumn wisdom,
spitting discarded leaves
as I pass in and under.

<113>

Ivy clings, too,
behind my bedroom.
Now, with my hyper ears
I hear them rustling,
even, at times,
when there is no breeze.
The vine is an on-ramp for spiders,
a ladder for spotted snakes.

And now, as sure
as I hear it,
I know the ivy is listening.
It knows the keystrokes
of my typewriter
and can read each letter
by its distinctive click.
It even knows the scratch
of my pen, can mouth
my words as fast as I write them.
Hedera helix, I write —
the tiny voice titters back
"English Ivy! Our proper name!"

The egg of All Saints
cracks into dawn.
Vine laps the sun-yolks,
tendrils exploring
new gaps in the masonry,
tilting vampire umbrellas
to the unsuspecting sun.

Smothering church and rectory,
carpeting the walls of the library,
cozying up the university halls,
the ivy horde is studying us,
always averting those
underleaf eyes, those
sharp little teeth.

<114>

They mean to kill us slowly,
urban piranha reducing
brownstones to dust,
churches to rubble,
pigeons to skeletons —
insidious vines,
    lethal creepers!

<115>

Nighters

RIDING THE BMT, ONE GAINS AN
empathy for freaks and underdogs,
a tolerance for rust and urine,
an intimate feel for shopping bags,
discarded styrofoam
and knotted twine.
   From three to dawn the Nighters rule,
roaming the moving trains,
always alert yet feigning sleep,
dark gods to whom
lost coins and buttons wend,
whom rapes propitiate,
gods of the snapping nerve.

Night train,
last train before the sunrise,
slows on Manhattan bridge,
five mile per hour maximum
on this shaky crossing,
trestles held up
with wood and prayers,
beams molting paint
to pitted rust holes.
I share the car
on the way to Brooklyn,
tired from my revels,
ignore the snaky-locked spinsters,
hoboes with canine teeth and paws,
the many-eyed jellyfish
whose tentacles turn and turn
the pages of tomorrow's
El Diario —

CUERPO SIN CABEZA
EN HUDSON!
screams the headline.

<116>

I watch a boy
unwittingly move in
from the adjacent car,
sprawl in the corner seat,
nodding to sleep.
I regard his cheeks,
his crimson lips,
promise of mustache,
sleek skin where neck
dips down in T-shirt,
glint of gold chain.
His hand drops,
blue veins
course down to palms,
a visible throb
at the dangling wrist.

The Nighters gather.
Rag-picking crones
spread oily tablecloth,
a Tarot deck,
a silver samovar,
two broken dinner plates.
Blind beggars hover
and block the doors —

the train, as though
by signal, slows to crawl,
to motionless —

we watch the sleeping youth,
he slumps, legs sprawled,
head to one side exposing
the copper expanse of throat —

<117>

The spinsters regard me.
"Broad back meat
is our bacon," one croons.
 "A tender thigh!"
her sister counters.
"A gullet of gore!"
    the dog-man howls,
"fill my paws
    with steaming innards!"

"Eyes!" cry the beggermen,
tapping their canes.
"Doe eyes brown
    and innocent!"
"Bones," say the jellyfish.
"Can't leave this train
without some vertebrae!"
I block their way,
push back
the fang and fork and scalpel,
scatter the monsters
into the hungry shadows.
I near the boy,
bend down to feel his breathing
a butterfly upon my fingers,
press myself over him —

"Blood," I say. "Blood."

<118>

He's Going to Kill Me Tonight

HE CANNOT SLEEP. HIS FEET
are cannonballs on creaking boards,
the wind's maniacal, the trees
a troop of palsied tap-
dancers on glass.
  His eyes lock-bolted awake
    his ears, electrified,
    are microphones
    set close to feedback screech.
In amber light of dusty lamp
    he reads the note
    that someone crammed
    under his door
in spidery script:
He's going to kill me tonight.

Midnight. The Reaper's shift begins.
The minute hand tips past Reason,
careens into Murder's tithe of night.
Somewhere a gloved hand
    drops bullets into grooves,
    revolves an oiled cylinder,
    tenses at trigger touch
Somewhere a knife attains
    its hair-split edge,
    rasping against stone,
    then like a snake
    into its coil'd hole,
    slithers into scabbard
From somewhere he hears these sounds
    (or doesn't hear them)

<119>

Who wrote the note? The blonde
on the floor below? Perhaps a pimp
she worked for has threatened her?
Perhaps a rescue and runaway in store?
He pictures the two of them in strange hotels
glued together on a blanket with spent passion.

But no, she moved a week ago. He groans
at the thought of the penthouse transvestite.
He calls her Desdemona — she's pasty pale —
the night watchman boyfriend beats her on Saturdays,
a noisy ritual for a weekend Othello.
Who else could it be?

The children's librarian in 19-A? (She tried
to get him to fix her stereo last week...)

He cannot guess who it is. The roaring truck
and raucous sanitation crew earthquake
and cymbal crash the building front, so loud
they would muffle a silenced gun, a choking,
the moan and gurgle of heart-stab mortality,
the fall of a chair beneath a noose.
He wonders if it happened just now.
He would never know until the newscast,
unless the squad cars clogged the pavement.
Which one? Which door would open on death?

2
Across the hall, the spinster lay in her bed,
breasts taut against the tightened sheets, hands
folded expectantly on throbbing heart.
She will be eighty-five next week.
Her knotted fingers wrote the warning note.

<120>

The window is open, the burglar gate unlatched,
the door unlocked and welcoming.
She waits for the man who is coming to kill her:
the grocer's boy, the laundry man, the super,
the mailman from Ponce, the plumber from Manila.
She waits for the man who is coming to save her:
the neighbor who smiles and helps her with packages.

The garbage truck covers his footsteps.
She grips starched sheets with painted nails.
The faces of killers and saviors begin to blur.

A streetwise silence sweeps after the garbage men,
sleek as the fur of an alleycat, stilling the air
save for the random scuttle of paper scraps, the roll
of soda cans, the rasp of a leaf against gutter,
the indefinable tread of the storm drain rats.
The wind invades the curtains, jostles her hair.
Her tears well up at the silence of fire escape.
No one has ever touched her.
No one ever will.

<121>

The Collectors

after Magritte

I know it *was* our father's house,
but prudence says he wouldn't mind
your packing up his legacies, a trunk
or two of city clothes, a photograph,
perhaps, of what had been a neighborhood
where now the sea laps barren beach
behind your yard. Do you enjoy the thought
that apple trees you climbed as a boy
are now the hanging place of cuttlefish?
Do you expect that whatever it is
that gobbles houses by night
and hauls the sidewalk off in chunks
will spare your little edifice?
I don't worry so much
about the lobsters, big as cows,
that made off with the Belgian clock,
the marble mantelpiece, or the horn
that I left in the attic; their taste
is too baroque to warrant another visit.
But I will prove, if I must
with photographs and measurements
that the oblong rock once half a mile
at sea will soon adorn the lawn,
then, with a nudge, the stairs;
next day it will bulge into the parlor;
and probably within a fortnight
sweep you a mile up the beach
to that stack of abandoned houses
where *it* has already assembled
what's left of the town.

<122>

It's one thing to be "lived through"
by Cosmic Consciousness,
serving some higher purpose as though
the Universe had plans, and we
were its chessmen. But this won't do,
this passive acceptance of
granite elbow-nudge,
this nibbling away at things,
reducing us to dust mite status
at the bottom of the vacuum bag!

Chain Smoker

From over his shoulder
    the old request,
  a querulous, "Cigarette?"
  "Oh, sure," he turns, a twirl
  of finger in pocket of shirt,
    then back with cigarette
    which is deftly removed by/
    He whirled to see whom,
saw only *what,* the smoking butt
that poised in air, joined now
by number two, lit by a flame
from something equally invisible.
Smoke seemed to respirate
into an indeterminate splotch
that might have been lungs,
then out again.
It stayed until dawn.
consuming a carton of filter tips
and a clutch of old cigars
before it coughed and was gone.

<123>

It's back again tonight,
dropping its ashes everywhere,
peril to curtains and furniture,
a glow and dim of double threat,
the one just lit, the other down
to the nub of the filter's edge.
It's not a poltergeist
but a habit whose owner renounced it,
a bodiless drift of repetition
too strong to dissipate
by merely yanking a body away
from beneath it;
when this incendiary guest descants,
will that be all, or is his house
a hostelry for disembodied urges,
where any old vice can find a vacancy?

<124>

The Sorcerer's Complaint

for Barbara Holland

No use deceiving her:
she spies the nightshade in my herbal;
skulks by when my illegal pet
happens to dangle a tangible limb
out and down the fire escape, three floors.
Swift-toed, she lifts the carpet up,
reads last night's chalked-in Pentagram;
turns in a fire alarm in jest
when my more musty conjurations
won't clear the chimney tops and gasp
out every window of my loft.
She's obstinate, turns up her furs
against the cloud that hovers there
on my command, that black
and personal drizzle that hounds
her Monday walks.

<125>

Unwelcome Company

Now cut that out! I've weathered a lot
of noise and discord in this urban arena:
the fenced-in barcarole of neighbor dogs,
the rising and falling of conga drums,
the melodious yowl of cats in heat,
gunshots or backfires, airplanes and trucks,
the swell and shudder made manifest
by continental drift — somehow I've slept
through all of that. Now it's *you*:

I've spied the rag and wraith of a banshee
before (one Hallow'd night I watched
one extricate itself from a tangle
of unyielding shrubs) but that was
you in the singular, your cry
dissolving in midnight wind.

This visitation is plural!
Two dozen hands, a whirl
of shrouds, a double dozen
of empty splotches for eyes,
and twelve cacophonous songs
battered by wingbeats into my window.

Who sent you? I'm not even Irish!
These whistles and yells can't be
intended for me. You have
the wrong address — the errant Kelly,
O'Brien, or Leary has moved.
The cat is Siamese, for God's sake!
Now gather up your dustmop heads
and flap off to somebody else's
premonition of death.
Silly birds!

<126>

The Dead End

FAR WEST, beyond the numbered avenues,
 there is a street,
  accessed by a curious courtyard,
 a peopled lane
  where lost on a moonlit but foggy night
you seem to know the passers-by.
House numbers seem too high,
 the street signs are illegible
but you feel recognized, and safe.
Each casual stroller,
 each idling window shopper
seems known to you.
They, for their part, impart a smile,
an instant's head-nod,
yet still pretend they do not know you.
And then it comes to you —
the vague acquaintances,
childhood friends you moved away from,
once-met and nearly forgotten lovers,
all of whom suddenly — or so they said —
just up and died.
You never saw a body.
The service was over before you heard.
The players reshuffled and life went on.
You never quite believed it, of course,
and now you have the proof:
they all just moved to this brick-lined street,
took up new names and furtive jobs
 caretaker, night watchman
 lobster shift foreman
 invisible cook in the diner kitchen
 night worker in office tower
unlisted phone, anonymous in nameless lodgings.

<127>

I found the street once, then lost it.
I've never managed to find it again,
can't help but wonder about those houses —
brownstones and bricks and a high-rise tower —
whose windows were those where curtains parted?
whose eyes, astonished, regarded me and pulled away?
Wish I could go up and read the nameplates,
knock on a certain door or two,
resume an interrupted dialogue,
give or receive an embrace
     I'm sorry I never shared.

But all too soon
     I'll be there anyway,
an anagram, a pseudonym,
a permanent resident
of Incognito Village

<128>

Curses!

EAR ME, BY THOTH,
by Tehuti the stylus-toothed!
Carry my song
on ibis wings.

This curse
I pen in black:
your name, dark Goddess,
in five hooked circles,

your properties
like hooded asps
in Coptic Greek —

My enemy must fall.
His picture burns
at circle's center —
we watch as
all but the eye
is consumed,
the *Ka* preserved —
perhaps some son of Set
already protects him!

Though some charm protects him,
twelve months from now
his grace year ends.
I'll burn the eye, then,
leave everything
to Fate.

<129>

If he has earned it
by some unlikely kindness,
my enemy is spared —
but if all who know him
suffer still, then take him,
dark, hungry belly
of the river bottom!

For him, no
coming forth by day,
not when the lowest workman
curses and spits
at hearing his name.

Save for him your
crocodile gnashing,
your behemoth
appetite,
your way
of making each human
morsel last!

I'll scatter the ash,
to give you his scent,
to break the line
between man and monster.
Rise from your sleep in the Nile,
span oceans with your hunger.
Find him, stalk him,
rend his dreams with your visage —

Hail and welcome Ammit,
Eater of the Dead!

<130>

The Grim Reaper

Paraphrase of an old German Folksong
"Es ist ein Schnitter, heisst der Tod"

There is a Reaper and his name is Death,
and though he kills, he kills for God,
and though his blade is sharpest of all
he stands at the wheel and whets it,
and when he is ready
    we must be ready, too.
O fair little flower, beware!

No matter what is green today,
the Reaper's scythe will mow away.
His blade never misses
  the noble Narcissus,
down from its plynth
  the lovely Hyacinth,
the Turk's Cap lilies fall —
harvested, all!
the meadows' roses dear
now toppled and sère.
O fair little sister, beware!

Will he take everything
  in sidelong swing
  of the blood-edged scythe?
While tulips are falling,
speedwell flying, blue tops
  into a bluer sky,
silver-fringed bluebells crying,
  doomed phlox not gold enough
  to ransom its beauty
against the swish, swish
of the Harvester.
O fair little brother, beware!

<131>

But now I defy you, Death!
Your holocaust night gives way to dawn.
I stand amid the scythe-cut lawn
and scorn your reaping. Pass by! pass by!
(But if you turn, and your red eye
turns back to seize me suddenly,
then mow me! take me away to be
the newest bloom in Death's dark flower pot,
a blossoming of interrupted thought,
deprived, yes! of pen and speech, and power,
but still I would defy you: no flower
of all earth's millions is the last!)
Be happy, my fair ones! Live on!

—The original German of this folksong was set by Brahms in his *German Folksongs for Four-Part Choir*. This paraphrase changes the original's rather conventional "die and go to Heaven" ending, and the poet has chosen to end each stanza with a different line rather than retaining the original refrain, "Beware, fair little flower!" The original song verse uses this refrain three times, and then "Be happy, fair little flower!" at the end.

<132>

The Ear Mound Shrine, Kyoto

1
Korea, 1597

Too many heads, my lord! Too many heads!
How to get home
   a hundred thousand
      of these Korean keepsakes?
Our ships are laden with gold and silver,
   jade and ceramics,
      inlaid cabinets,
         silks and scrolls.
If we leave them behind, my lord,
   the men will be furious.
We have to prove the extent of our triumph.
Our honor is at stake.

We have burned their palaces,
   looted their pathetic little temples,
turned all their mansions to ash,
   squeezed the last coins
from the rural landlords,

but we shall all be seen
   as idle braggarts,
robbers of tombs and empty houses,
unless we pile the skulls
at Toyotomi's feet.
What will the general say?

The leader deliberates,
talks with his captains
of ballast and measures,
the weight of captives,
then calls his men
to the hilltop tent.

<133>

Cut off the ears,
    he tells them.
We'll give the general
    a mountain of ears.
If ears are already missing,
    we'll take the noses.

As for the rotting heads —
line them up
    along the sea-cliff.
Let them face east,
    eyes wide,
    mouths open
in suitable terror,
a warning to all
of our superior power.
Drink to the general —
a thousand years
to Toyotomi Hideyoshi!

2
Japan, 1598

The ladies lounge
in the treasure chamber.
Look what Hideyoshi brought us!
They test the furniture,
line up the vases —
    these for spring,
    these for autumn —
chitter with laughter
at pornographic scrolls.
Do Korean women really do that?

Their fluttering robes
    and cherry-stained lips,
their dancing fingers
    and playful eyes

<134>

ignore the line of captives
seated on wooden benches
before the general's chamber.
More Koreans pass through daily —
    women for the taking
     for a life of kitchen labor,
sad old scholars
    with mandarin whiskers
destined to tutor
    the general's nephews,
rosy-cheeked boys
    for the monks
      and opera masters.

There is another room
for Hideyoshi's use only.
What does he do
    in the "Chamber of Ears"?
The servants say
    the smell is terrible,
       flies and rats everywhere.
Not even burning camphor
    can mask its charnel aroma.

They know he requisitioned urns,
    boxes and baskets of all dimensions;
they know that thousands of ears
    are piled in pyramids
    from which they tumble daily,
each fleshy nautilus tilted
    a different way.
The general arranges them for hours —
    something not right
      about an inverted ear, he says.
He thinks of sorting lefts and rights —
    what odds against
       the reuniting of ear lobes
         of just one victim?

<135>

This has been going on for months.
Not one of the concubines
     has gotten pregnant
          since the ears were delivered,
               and the soldiers rewarded.
If this goes on, what of the dynasty?
A servant tells the oldest wife:
     It can't go on. He'll tire of it.
     The ears are black and shrunken now
     like poison mushrooms.

The general stops speaking
     to his subordinates, calls in
a scribe to issue written orders.
I am spied upon, he tells his minister.

Toyotomi's nights
     are not given to slumber.
He spends three days
     in the Chamber of Ears,
comes out white-haired
     and foaming at the mouth.
Fever's bed claims him.

The ears, it seems,
     have been *listening.*
The general has good ears, too.
He knows that something fleshy
     fumbles about in there —
and not a rat — one living ear,
or a pair of them,
among two hundred thousand dead ones,
spying his words, his plans,
waiting to fly on ghost wings
to the Korean fleet,
     to tell Admiral Yi,
          his nemesis,
of every weakness.

<136>

Before he dies
   in a black-face fever,
with trembling hands,
   throat choking
as though pressed down
by invisible stones,
Toyotomi utters his final order:
Bury the ears! All of them!
Put a stone shrine above them.
Guard the place. Let nothing escape.

3
The Ear Mound Shrine, Kyoto, 1998

Caretaker, gardener,
shrine attendant,
one old man of eighty,
sweeps up the cigarette butts
a careless wind deposits
at the base of the Ear Mound.

A plaque commemorates
the ancient invasion
four hundred years ago,
   the massacre,

<137>

the burial of Korean ears
in hopes of placating
the angry spirits.

It is silent here in Kyoto,
the odd stillness of tree and stone,
the looming, stark monument —
more than silent, I think.
This place takes in sound.
It is *listening.*
It would hear a whisper,
a wish in the subconscious.

There is an annual ceremony, I am told,
a burning of incense,
a proper prayer.
But is it heard across the water?
Tenfold ten thousand ghosts
gasp on the Korean seashore,
waiting for apologies they cannot hear,
scanning the east
   with doleful demon eyes,
ghost hands on their
   ever-bleeding cheeks,
mouths still open.

The place asks: Have you learned?
Does life still sever life?
Is the thread from sire to son
to be left unbroken now?

At dawn, the raked earth
stirs around the monument.
The tiny pebbles levitate,
grooves, channels, wormholes
into the ancient mound
push out like tiny volcanoes.
Then hordes of pink antennae
burst out at the trumpeting sun.

<138>

One hundred thousand
hatching butterflies!
Clouds of pink and salmon,
   vermilion and cherry,
spread their matched wings
   in endless mutation,
whirlwind of cho-cho maidens,
    warrior moths,

mandarin and concubine,
scholar, musician — all butterflies,
glyphs on their wings
   of all the ancient families,

ascending on an updraft,
cloud of every color
   heading westward,
    westward to sing
to the ghosts who called them.

<139>

The New Tenant

It's silent below
in the Army/Navy warehouse
when the second-floor tenant
tunes up his tweeters,
fires up the thunder
of a mammoth subwoofer.
(Dim-lit, mouse quiet, the attic's
an atelier of art school women,
bed squeaks, drain gurgles,
keys in the lock
their only aural assertion.)

On Floor Two it's Beethoven:
Egmont and Equestrian Marches,
answered from below
by jackboots *ein-zwei* goose-stepping,
old army uniforms'
starched arms saluting.

When it's the *Marseillaise* above,
a hundred French sailor suits,
enfants de la Patrie,
fly from their hangers below,
and flap an apache dance
against the window panes.
(A teapot whistle,
summarily stifled,
a stainless steel spoon
clabbering porcelain
the only sounds
from the attic.)

<140>

On Shostakovich night
the orchestra thunders:
below, old Stalin medals
and Lenin pins skitter,
while *CCCP* tee-shirts
puff up angrily.

A Russian army greatcoat
stuffs its pockets
with an ever-growing list
of local citizens
with anti-People tendencies.
(The attic is dark
as a desanctified belfry.)

When he crescendos up
to the *1812 Overture*,
trunk-tops flip open below:
landmines and hand grenades
roll about aimlessly,
their impotent collisions
no match for cannons,
the clangor of church bells.
(While "Bowling for Hitler"
plays on the floor below,
the artists above
tip-toe in fur-lined slippers,
each in her own I-pod,
ear-bud solipsism.

On a more somber night
he has tea and listens
to Britten's *War Requiem*.
A solemn tramping erupts
onto the stairwell.

<141>

There is a knock. He looks
into an eyeless socket,
a leering skull,
an armless doughboy jacket,
not one, but the first
of a long line
of crutched and crippled
soldier semblances.

"Pucelles?" the coat-ghost asks.
"Frauleins? Girls?"
Cocking an ear
to the faintest sound
of a hair dryer,
the tenant points upward.
The tramp-tread of dead boots
mounts to the third floor.

The art school girls
have visitors.

<142>

The Black Huntsman

(after Victor Hugo's *Le chasseur noir*)

Who goes there? You, passer-by,
why choose these somber woods,
vast crowds of crows a-flutter —
no place to be with a rainstorm coming!"

"Make way! I am the one
who moves in shadow.
Make way! — for the Black Huntsman!"

The leaves on the trees,
    which the wind has stirred,
are whistling, and I have heard
that all this forest
    will be ashiver with shrieks
when the storm-cloud clears
and the moon shines down
on the Witches' Sabbath!

Why tarry here? Go chase the doe,
run down the fallow deer,
out of the forest to the unplowed fields.
And more than deer: this is your night
to bag a Tsar, or at least,
an archduke of Austria,
    O Black Huntsman!

The leaves on the trees —
    Hasten, Black Huntsman,
    to sound your horn-call,
    fasten your leggings
    for a long ride.
    The easy stag who comes grazing
    in plain sight by the manor?

<143>

Ah, no, ride down the King,
ride down a Bishop or two,
   Black Huntsman!

The leaves on the trees —
   It rains, the thunder
   roars, the flood
   sends rivers raging.
   Refuge engulfed, the fox
   flees this way, that way,
   no shelter anywhere, no hope!

   Take not the easy prey:
   there goes a spy on horseback,
   there a judge in his carriage —
      take *them*, Black Huntsman!

The leaves on the trees —
   Do not be moved
   by those monastic flutterings
   in the wild oat-fields,
   those spasms of St. Anthony's
      Satanic possession.
   Hunt down the abbot,
   spare not the monk,
      O Black Huntsman!

The leaves on the trees—
   Your hounds are on the scent.
   Go for the bears;
   leave no wild boar unslaughtered.
   And while you're at it,
   doing what you do so well,
   Black Huntsman,
   hunt down the Pope, the Emperor!

<144>

The leaves on the trees —
    The wily wolves side-step you,
    so loose the pack upon them.
    A stream! The track is lost
    in a teeming waterfall.
    But what is this? An ex-president
    without his secret service men!
    And there in that cave,
    a former vice-president cowering!
    Run, hounds! Bring them to ground!
        Well done, O Black Huntsman!

The leaves on the trees,
    which the wind has stirred
    are falling, and I have heard
    that the dark Sabbath
    with all its raucous shrieks
    has fled the forest.
    The cloud is pierced
    by the cock's bright crow:
    the dawn is here!

All things regain their original force.
My nation becomes herself again,
    so beautiful to behold,
a white archangel robed in light,
    even to you, Black Huntsman!

The leaves on the trees,
    which the wind has stirred
    are falling, and I have heard
    that the dark Sabbath
    with all its raucous shrieks
    has fled the forest.
    The cloud is pierced
    by the cock's bright crow:
    the dawn is here!

From Victor Hugo's *Chatiments: "Le Chasseur noir"*

<145>

DIE LAUGHING

Valkyries on Route 128

ABOUT THOSE THREE BLONDES
in a convertible —
a red one that wings on the six-lane thruway,
a blood-red Chevy that seems to leap
the concrete barriers, weaving the maze
of plastic cones and flares and flashers
without a dent or mishap. They never
turn off at a cloverleaf or pay a toll.
No one has ever seen them at Ho-Jo's.
Lately they've started arriving at accidents,
pull men and boys from their flaming cars,
drape bone-broken bodies across the hood
(some dead, some moaning in final agony,
all in the prime of their youth and beauty,
death-clenched hands around bottles and cans).
No one knows where they take them.
Tourists see them with their bloody trophies,
hear strains of Wagner doppler by,
yet minutes later they can't be found
by any convergence of patrol car,
roadblock or chopper on radio alert.
CB truck drivers report more sightings
before or after a major collision.
The police are understandably perplexed.

<146>

The McWilliams' Coffee Table

O THE JONESES WENT OUT AND DID IT:
took truck and winch and crowbar
and lifted a lamb-adorned
delicate gravestone
from country burial ground,

washed dirt and roots from its base,
set it on oak frame and casters
to be the life of parties,
the butt of jokes, the putting
down place of soda cans, iced tea
and sweating daiquiri glasses.
Wine stains the pearly limestone.
Nicotine marks will not clean off.
The floorboards beneath
give off an ominous groan.

Torn between envy and outrage,
the neighbor couple lingers and gawks.
Mrs. McWilliams wants to report them
to the town and parish authorities.
Her husband Peter writes down the name,
Lilian McHenry, who died in 18-
something, listens again as drunken Jones
retells the hazards of late night
shopping, guesses the town
where he made the heist.
"Hard work — and dangerous,"
McWilliams speculates.
"Like candy from babies," Jones boasts.

A new moon comes and passes.
It's party time at the McWilliamses
And what should the startled visitors
find sporting a Chinese vase,
a *Vanity Fair* and a plate of brie?

<147>

An oblong box of Plexiglas
extending the length of the oversize sofa,
contains a sleeping beauty occupant —
none other than Lilian McHenry,
exhumed with care from her stoneless plot,
her long white corpse hair intact,
her long nails black, eye sockets
dark as six-foot soil,
her shroud a study in tatters,
nose gone, gap teeth a hideous smile,
an onyx ring on her skeleton fingers.

Guests circle it cautiously,
noses alert for that certain smell,
eyeing the carpet for telltale stains,
dreading the thought of a sudden motion
within the grip-lock of polymer.
Soon enough the discomfort is over.
Lilian is adorned with coffee rings,
a spill of gin, a cocaine dusting.
The Jones parties are a thing of the past.
The McWilliamses so chic and clever,
so *au courant* in the finer art
of interior decoration.

<148>

Knecht Ruprecht, or, The Bad Boy's Christmas

DON'T EVEN THINK OF CALLING YOUR
    mother or father.
They can't hear you.
No one can help you now.
I came through the chimney
  in the form of a crow.

You're my first this Christmas.
You're a very special boy, you know.
You've been bad,
bad every day,
dreamt every night
    of the next day's evil.
It takes a lot of knack
    to give others misery
for three hundred and sixty
consecutive days!
How many boys have you beaten?
How many small animals killed?
Half the pets in this town
    have scars from meeting you.
Am I Santa Claus? *Cack, ack, ack!*
Do I look like Santa, you little shit?
Look at my bare-bone skull,
  my eyes like black jelly,
  my tattered shroud.
My name is Ruprecht,
    Knecht Ruprecht.
I'm Santa's cousin! *Cack, ack, ack!*

<149>

Stop squirming and listen —
(of course I'm hurting you!)
I have a lot of visits to make.
My coffin is moored to your chimney.
My vultures are freezing their beaks off.

But as I said, you're special.
You're my number one boy.
When you grow up,
you're going to be a noxious skinhead,
    maybe a famous assassin.
Your teachers are already afraid of you.
In a year or two you'll discover girls,
a whole new dimension of cruelty and pleasure.
Now let's get down to business.
Let me get my bag here.
Presents? Presents! *Cack, ack, ack!*
See these things? They're old,
old as the Inquisition,
make dental instruments look like toys.

No, nothing much, no permanent harm.
I'll take a few of your teeth,
then I'll put them back.
This is going to hurt. There —
the clamp is in place.
Let's see — where to plug in
those electrodes?

Oh, now, don't whimper and pray to God!
As if you ever believed in God! *Cack, ack, ack!*
I know every tender place in a boy's body.
There, that's fine! My, look at the blood!
Look at the blood! Look at the blood!

<150>

You'll be good from now on? That's a laugh.
Am I doing this to teach you a lesson?
I am the Punisher. I do this
because I enjoy it! I am just like you!
There is nothing you can do.
I can make a minute of pain seem like a year.
No one will ever believe you.

Worse yet, you cannot change.
Tomorrow you will be more hateful than ever.
The world will wish you had never been born.

Well now, our time is up. Sorry for the mess.
Tell your mother you had a nosebleed.
Your father is giving you a hunting knife
for which I'm sure you'll have a thousand uses.

Just let me lick those tears from your cheeks.
I love the taste of children's tears.
My, it's late! Time to fly! *Cack, ack, ack!*
I'll be back next Christmas Eve!

Knecht Ruprecht, from German folklore, is St. Nicholas' evil twin, who
punishes bad children.

<151>

Christmas Verses

CHRISTMAS DINNER
Spoiled meat and green potatoes,
Sour milk and black tomatoes,
All mixed in with something found
Sprouting from a graveyard mound.
Don't eat Grandma's mushroom stew,
If you know what's good for you!

THE ASPIC
Aunt Molly's aspic just sits and glistens.
It's back every year, untasted, untried.
She begs us to taste, but no one listens,
Observing the mummified mouse inside.

THE CHRISTMAS TREE
Fall to the carpet! Cover your head!
Go up the stairs and keep to your bed!
There'll be no presents for us to see —
There's a rabid bat in the Christmas tree!

A DECEMBER CUSTOM
When Sarah wanted the men to kiss her,
She stood just where they couldn't miss her.
She took them all beneath the door —
Yet none of them came back for more.
The moral's plain—it only figures —
The mistletoe was full of chiggers.

<152>

OUR HUNTING FATHERS
The snow was white, the snow was red,
When hunters shot the reindeer dead.
They tossed the sleigh into the lake.
Hoping to hide their worst mistake,
They torched the old fart in his crimson suit,
Opened his bags and divided the loot

JINGLE BELLS
Carolers came to the end of the lane
(They thought they'd cheer the widower Miller).
If only they'd known the old man was insane,
Dreaming the dreams of a serial killer.
He asked them in for some Christmas cheer,
Plied them with candy and soda and beer.
They stayed and they laughed till they almost cried,
Then choking on poison they promptly died.

APPALACHIAN MARY
O wonder of wonders! O day so lucky!
The Virgin Mary will visit Kentucky!
I hear an angel crying, "Hark!
See Mary's face in that twisted bark!"
"No — there she is! — and I'm no fool —
Behold her eyes in the swimming pool!"
"No, here! No, here! Come see it, please —
Her folded hands in this moldy cheese!"
"T-shirts! T-shirts! Buy souvenirs
Before the apparition disappears!"

THE GROWTH
The growth on Uncle Abner's wife
    has everyone alarmed —
She's going for the surgeon's knife
    but we want the THING unharmed!

<153>

SILENCE

The new baby's cries could be heard from afar.
It pierced ever ear, though no door was ajar.
We closed every window to block the wailing
but cotton and earplugs were unavailing.

Then Uncle Abner could bear it no more.
He went through the Williamsons' unlocked door
and dropped a bell jar over the thing.

It could howl, it could scream,
  it could bellow or sing,
but the sound was no more than a muffled din,
as its air grew stale, and its oxygen thin.

<154>

The Anaconda Poems

COIL 1: REINCARNATION
Some want to come back from death,
    reliving their human folly
        again and again,
life after dreary life
until they get it right,
then slide down the chute
        to soulless oblivion.

We who don't care for perfection
are doomed to come back as animals.
                    Do we return
    according to our habits,
        the heaped accounts of karma,
or can we choose?

I choose,
    study the animal kingdom
        for the soul's best condo,
                    the leafiest turf,
        the longest return engagement.
    Choosing is hard for a hermit poet.
            No herd instinct for me,
        no hive or flock or pride
                if you please.
Let me be something
    solitary yet strong,
lordly and unapproachable.
I search for incarnations
on top of the food chain.
            I'll eat
    but not be eaten
hunt but elude the hunter.

At last I find it —
    the giant anaconda.

<155>

Female I'll have to be —
　　the males are nothing.

　　　　Mother of all snakes,
　　　　　　I'll grow to thirty feet,
　　　　　　spend all day lazing
　　in the waters of the Amazon.
　　　　Nights I'll wait
　at the edge of the river,
when deer and rabbit,
panther and lemur
come to drink.
My fangs attach
　to whatever approaches;
　　　I throw my coils
　　　　with amazing speed.
　　　　　The astonished prey
　　　　　　immobile, breathless
　　　　　　　as I squeeze　squeeze
　　　　　　　　　　　　squeeze
　　　　　　to heartstop stillness.
　　　Compacted to sausage shape
　　　　the still warm animals
　　　slide down my gullet,
my inward turning teeth
guiding them onwards.

I have no enemies,
　　swim unconcerned
　　　　among piranha
　　　　　　electric eels
　　　　and crocodile caymans.
　　　　　　Not even my prey
　　　　　seem to notice me
　　　as I mount skyward
to the treetop banquet,
my green and black camouflage
　　　matching the dappled forest.

<156>

Parrots and toucans
　　　I eat like candy.

Only the monkeys fear me
　　　somersault screaming
　　　at the sight of me —
　　Oh, and the hairless apes
　　　in the jungle villages:
　　I need but show my tongue,
　　　my unblinking eye,
　　　to make them run away.

　　Taking the sun
　　on a bank aburst
　　with yellow blossoms
　I am a jasmine empress
　　　irresistible
　to the males of my species.
　I sense them coming,
　feel the grass parting,
　　a dozen today
　twining about me.
　I turn with them,
　move toward mud.
Hours we　　　coil together —
　puny　　　　as they are it
feels good　　　everywhere —
one of them　　will find the spot.

COIL 2: ANACONDA IN NEW YORK

I stow away
  on an airplane's cargo hold,
    emerge at La Guardia,
      hitch ride on a luggage rack
   through tunnel to Manhattan.
I mean to eat my way around —
  a big green worm
     in the big green Apple!

City Hall park has plenty of trees,
pigeons abounding.
  I study the populace,
    learn how to move among them
     with camouflage and mimicry.
       This is going to be easy.
   I will have my fill of man-food.

   Homeless Anaconda
   a garbage bag
  unraveled to wrap me
gets me a night
in the city shelter
(lots to eat
but it needed washing)

  Hip-Hop Anaconda,
   plenty of room for me
    in those baggy pants.
     Ate well on 125th Street
      but had to spit out
     gold chains and a boom box.

     Transvestite Anaconda
     prowling the piers
    in matching alligator
   accessories. Honey
  I could just eat you alive.

<158>

An Anaconda Dowager
    draped in furs
    indulging my sweet
        incisors
      with the ladies
      at Rumpelmeyers.

      Roller Blade Anaconda
        knocking down doormen
            on Central Park South,
           scarfing up poodles
            at the curbside.

           Painted purple,
        welcomed as Barney,
     I am Day Care Anaconda,
      turning a jungle gym
      into my cafeteria
    (I really must start
counting calories!)

I'm unadorned as
    Bowery Anaconda —
      an hallucination —
        acquiring a taste
          for marinated men
            left out for the taking
              in cardboard boxes!

        The Anaconda Nun
        in her floppy habit
      waylays worshipers
    in the nave of St. Patrick's.
      Irish O'Connor
wouldn't know a snake
If he saw one.

<159>

Now I am
Steam Tunnel Anaconda
   need time to digest
      all my victims
         time to prepare
            for the progeny
               already swelling in my belly.

         I'll winter here in warmth,
            no rent   no taxes,
         won't need a green card
            welfare or Medicaid
         They can't zoo or jail me
            I have immunity
         endangered species status.

         When my seventy-five babies
         emerge from   manhole covers
         on Easter   morning
         on lower   Fifth Avenue
         they'll already   be citizens—
         American   Anacondas!

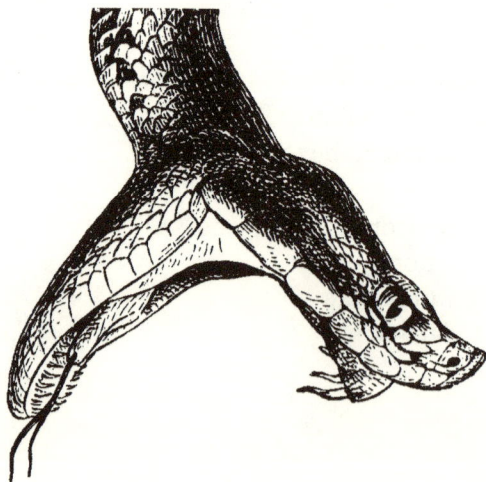

<160>

Gorgon at the Wedding

OME WEDDING, OUR DAUGHTER'S!
the garden's a shambles
the groom in a state of
the bride hysterical
and all because of those Greeks
on Mother's side.
I said the wedding list
was dangerous —
too many *ioses*
and *opouloses,*
too many guests
without extending it
into the mythical.

For an Episcopal affair
you dredged up every uncle,
every conceivable cousin,
till trunk lines swelled
with reservations.
They might have come in chariots,
sky cars and dragonback
if I hadn't finally
cried *Enough!*

Then Auntie Eu arrived:
frail bird of a woman,
a shipping magnate's widow
rowed into Newport harbor
on some antique trireme.
She stood in the tent,
her chiton flapping,
pecking at hors d'oeuvres,
bony at elbow and ankle
in that unthinkable turban.

<161>

Auntie Eu! you shrieked,
presenting the groom and bride
  Auntie Eu — Evelyn
  Auntie Eu — Jack

You chattered on
about her home in Greece,
  her hobby,
those charming little
marble animals
frozen as if in life.
They're all the rage
at the shops in the Agora.

How like an aging movie star
  she seemed then,
her green black aviators
like eyes on a praying mantis,
Casino waiters fawning,
all eyes upon her jewelry,
vast crowds crashing
the mansion party
to say they'd been

If only poor Jack,
just seeking a toilet,
had but the sense to knock
before he stumbled in
to where poor Auntie Eu
at bathroom mirror
was tucking her snakes
into her turban folds —

if only his sense
had told him to run
instead of to freeze,
that startled instant
before she turned
just might have saved him.

<162>

He cried out "Snay —! Snay —!"
She turned. She gave him
her best hard glance.

So now the wedding's off,
    for how does Evelyn
    confess to poor Jack
our curious lineage.
She can't —
          he's petrified.

The Gorgon Medusa had two sisters, Euryale and Stheno, who survived her,
eternally mourning her murder by Perseus. The direct glance of any of the three
Gorgons can turn men to stone.

<163>

The Sailor and the Oak Nymphs

AK WITH ITS ROOTS IN CORE OF IRON,
lava-tipped fingers reaching to magma,
ancient beyond the reckoning of sun,
brown as the acorn egg that bore her,
branches tightened, taut as muscles
boles a gnarl of screaming faces
echoes of strange births
and even stranger lovers.

Her skin bears scars:
   the nettling name of some boy,
the pen-knifed initials of lovers
who long ago subsumed
      into the blur of humus,
the signature of a deeper attack,
knife-thrust of a drunken sailor
who slashed at her one moon-mad night,
breaking through bark to cambium.

She was a long time healing,
but years before the gashes stitched
to spiderlines

they found the man in a nearby wood
   anonymous cadaver
   throat slit by self
   or by an unknown hand.

Knowing this oak,
I know how he came to be there,
I need but taste the tannin
of my October cup, but close
my eyes to see the tale unravel:

<164>

First came the virgin girl,
the gentle Amaltheia,
the tender one who lured him
before the tavern door,
offered him kisses, promised
to walk with him
in slanted light of the forest.

He waited not far from the bleeding oak.
The fair one broke her promise.
He cursed her, wished for the warmth
    of the familiar dives,
    the hot wet swallow
    of burning whiskey.

And then a lusty nymph appeared,
red-lipped in leather,
a slut who said her name was Io.
Io was inexhaustible
fulfilling his every fantasy,
urging, then teasing,
then turning to mockery

of his all too human manhood.
Failing to please her,
he rolled away from her,
drifted into an angry stupor.

He lay half-dressed,
disheveled, undignified,
not hearing the flight of Io,
the leaf-crunch arrival
    of the barefoot hag,
the autumn crone, oak-born
Adrasteia, the unavoidable.

Before he could rise
from the cold-wet leaf bed,
she leaped on him,

<165>

her bony knees on his shoulders
breasts dry and pendant
    through tattered nightgown,
nipples like withered twigs
hair limp and gray
    and knotted with burrs,
her breath as she kissed him
the scent of apple rot,
the hint of something dead
turned up beneath wet leaves.

Her cracked voice whispered
the song the oak tree taught her:
of the hundred-handed slayers
  who sharpened knives in caves,
of the red-fanged worms
  burrowing up to find him,
of the arctic wind unleashed
  to follow him everywhere
  like a personal blizzard.

Then she was gone. He lay
beneath a tilted moon,
  a mocking Venus,
dry-mouthed and aching
with the bite of frost.
He found his pockets emptied,
wallet and coins,
greenbacks among the soggy leaves
his pocket knife,
his comb,
his fine-honed shaving razor
  already open
blade gleaming on a blood red banner,
the singing leaf of the oak tree.

<166>

End of the World

OT WITH A TRUMPET
but a whisper. No angels
proclaimed the end. Prophets
with sandwich signs
did not predict it.
No tea-leaf ladies
or noted astrologers
knew that the end would come
at half-past eight
in the morning.

It was a Monday,
(of all days!)
catching them dressed
for their funerals.

Who would have guessed
that this October,
instead of leaves
the people turned
and blew away,
that gravity,
the faithful plodder,
would take a holiday?

First some commuters
on a platform in Connecticut
fell straight into a cloudless sky
trying to hook
to lampposts and poles
with flailing arms.

Even the oversize stationmaster
was not immune,
hung by his fingertips
to shingled roof,

<167>

an upside-down balloon.
His wig fell down,
the rest of him
shot shrieking upwards.
Slumlords in Brooklyn
dropped rent receipts,
clutched hearts and wallets
as they exfoliated,
burst into red and umber explosions
and flapped away.

A Senator stepped down
from his bulletproof limo,
waved to the waiting lobbyist,
  (sweaty with suitcase
   full of hundreds)
only to wither to leaf-brown dust,
crumbling within his overcoat.

Stockbrokers adjusted their power ties,
buttoned their monogrammed blazers,
pushed one another from narrow ledge
falling from Wall Street precipice
into the waiting sky,
printouts and ticker tapes,
class rings and credit cards
feathering back down.

Bankers turned yellow,
wisped out like willow leaf
from crumpled pin-stripe,
filling the air
with streamers of vomit
as they passed the roof
of the World Trade Center.

<168>

The colors were amazing:
black women turned ivory,
white men turned brown and sere,
athletes swelled up
    to fuchsia puffballs,
Chinese unfurled
    to weightless jade umbrellas.

Winds plucked the babies from carriages,
oozed them out of nurseries,
pulled them from delivery rooms,
from the very womb —
gone on the first wind out and upwards.

The great horde filled the stratosphere
darkened the jet stream,
too frail to settle in orbit,
drifting to airless space.

They fell at last into the maw
of the black hole Harvester,
a gibbering god
    who made a bonfire
    of the human host
the whirling spiral of skeletons
a rainbow of dead colors
red and yellow and black and brown
    albino and ivory
parched-leaf skins a naked tumble.

The bare earth sighed.
Pigeons took roost in palaces.
Tree roots began
the penetration of concrete.
Rats walked the noonday market.

<169>

Wild dogs patrolled
  the shopping malls.
Wind licked at broken panes.
A corporate logo toppled
  from its ziggurat.
Lightning jabbed down
  at the arrogant churches
  abandoned schools
  mansions unoccupied
started a firestorm
a casual blaze
as unconcerned
as that unfriendly shrug
that cleaned the planet.

<170>

Squanto's Wind

A ruffian wind
content till now to move
through barricades of steel
to tug of sea,
forgetful of forest and creek,
rears up at last,
howls *No* emphatically

at the Hancock tower,
a block as gray as greed,
lunging from bedrock to sky.

The primal *No* acquires more force,
plucks glass like seeds
from a ruptured grape.

The window panes explode —
a million shards
of architectural sneeze
scattered by gravity
to punctuate the streets
with gleaming arrowheads,
obsidian spears,
black tomahawks
of dispossession.

What Manitou is this
who shakes his fist
at the barons of finance?
Whatever happened to
"Welcome, Englishmen!"
(the first words spoken
by Native to Puritan)?

<171>

The engineers move in,
revise their blueprints
while covered walkways
protect pedestrians
from Hancock's continued
defenestration.

Months pass, and yet
a lingering wind remains,
circling the sheltered walks,
lapping at plywood sheets,
a sourceless gale
that ruffles Bostonians

with its reiterated cry,
not on this land you don't.

On really windy days
the whole tower sways
and workers turn green
from motion sickness.
Millions are spent
on a countersliding bed
of lubricated lead
to gyro the floor to apparent
stillness; millions more
from the slap-suited builders
on fifteen hundred tons
of diagonal braces,
all to to stop
the whole ziggurat
from an inevitable topple, should
just one wind, at just one angle
bring everything
in a snarl of pretzeled girders.
Finally all ten thousand panes
are one by one, removed
and one by one replaced.

<173>

Is Squanto satisfied
that the tower was sold,
that the new owners slid
to bankruptcy (at least
on paper), though bankers slide
from one debacle to another
and earn baronial bonuses?

No! His feathered face frowns
on clouded-over golf days.
His never-tiring gusts divert
the errant baseball, ensuring
decades of home-game dejection.

It will take more than
double-dug foundations,
wind-tunnel-tested
new window panes,
to still these vectors of rage.

Token pow-wows at shopping malls
and suburban parks
do not fool old Squanto:
sharp-dealing and inhospitable,
Boston must pay!

<174>

Autumn on Mars

for Ray Bradbury

On Mars the black-trunked trees are dense
with summer's crimson foliage.
When dry-ice autumn comes,
the oaks singe sickly green.
The land is a riot of airborne olive,
    chartreuse and verdigris,
green fire against a pink and cloudless sky.
The sour red apples go yellow sweet;
the wind-blanched wheat
    forsakes its purple plumage;
cornstalks are tied in indigo bundles;
eyes flicker ghoulishly
    as candles are set
        in carved-out green gourds.

Grandfathers warn their terrified children
of the looming, ominous blue planet,
roiled with thunderclouds and nuclear flashes,
that warlike, funeral-colored Earth
from which invaders would one day come,
decked in the somber hues of death,
withered and green like dead-pile leaves,
armed to the hilt with terrible weapons.

"I've seen them!" an elder asserts.
"They have two eyes, flat on their heads!"
Eye stalks wiggle in disbelief.
"They walk on two legs, like broken sticks!"
Multi-jointed leglets thump in derision.
"They speak in the animal octave,
    and they bark like krill-dogs."
The children shriek in red and purple.
"No way, Old One! Don't make us think it!
How can they talk without twinkling?"

<175>

"Their rockets go higher with every turn
    of our world around the life-star.
Earthers will come, thick on the ground
    like our thousand-year mugworms.
They will kill us, take our females captive,
burn our egg domes, eat our aphidaries!"

A fireball slashes the pink horizon.
Two hundred eye-stalks follow the arc.
"That might be one of their robots now!
Their probes are watching everywhere!"
Now fifty Martian youngsters scream,
shrieking in ultraviolet tones,
crab legs scattering in every direction.

The Old Ones smile in five dimensions,
sit down for a cup of hot grumulade
and some well-earned peace and quiet.
"It's not nice to frighten the young ones,"
the eldest muses, "but it wouldn't be autumn
without a little Halloween."

<176>

Diagnosis of E.A. Poe

Poe, rabid? Never!
A doctor avers
from a yellow medical chart
that Edgar died
in Baltimore,
not in the drunk
delirium
of the election night gutter,

not walked like a zombie
from poll to tavern,
tavern to poll,
signing ballots in shaking hand
as Edgar Montresor
and Allan Pym,
Hop-Frog De La Poer
and Edgardo Prospero —

no, not this,
but a terminal case
of *rabies.*

The question is
what bit him?
Was it a fleeting bat,
a crouching wolf
in some graveyard,
a foaming-mouth hound
at the tavern door,

a squirrel
he reached out to feed,
ungrateful!

<177>

Or out of the inky night
did a red-eyed raven
descend, raking its claws,
its unforgiving beak
across his forehead?

Poe, rabid? Never!
He was immune, I say!
He had the scars
of wounds long healed —
the pestilential bite
of the critics,
of his Judas Reverend
Griswold,
the lamprey fangs
of New York lady poets.

Note: After Poe was driven out of New York society by squabbling admirers, and
after the New York poetesses interfered in his courtship of Sarah Helen
Whitman, a Providence poet and eligible widow, Poe disowned them all, writing,
"I shall forever shun the pestilential society of lady poets."

<178>

Here at the Point

Secret transcript of a meeting of The Security Committee of Swan Point Cemetery

ERE AT THE POINT
we tolerate no nonsense.
Let the word go out
to the security guards:

photographing the monuments
is not permitted,
especially at Lovecraft's grave.

Families spend thousands
to put these obelisks and stones,
statues and mausoleums
onto our grounds

to be seen here.
Here! not in some smelly
newspaper!

If artists show up
with paints and easels,
they can depict the foliage,
but not the monuments,
not the monuments!

Use your judgment, men.
If one of those Art Club Ladies
sets up to paint, just shoo
her off politely.

<179>

But if it's a RISD[1] kid —
one of those green-haired,
snot-nosed spray painters
from the Design School,
a little ride over
to the *trespasser's shed*
might be in order.

TV crews
are absolutely prohibited —
escort them right back
to the outer gates.

As always, no picnicking!
No food or drink
whatsoever — last month
we had a whole family
eating at a graveside
(damn Armenians!).
We stopped that in a hurry.

You can't let up,
not for a moment.
Watch for those kids,
keep an eye peeled
for lurkers, and *couples*.

Matthewson here keeps a graph
of how many conundrums
we find, and where —

conundrums, you know,
those little rubber things —
disgusting!

---

[1] RISD. Rhode Island School of Design.

<180>

This is a place of repose.
Repose. Why don't they get it?
No eating, no drinking,
no urinating, no fornicating,
no congregating.

Those Lovecraft fans
are the worst. Reading their poetry,
mouthing what rituals
we can only imagine —
what the hell is *Cthulhu fhthagn*, anyway?

That Rutherford person
and those evil twins
dressed up as Lovecraft
or monks or ravens —
they have to be stopped!
Why doesn't someone stop them?

And look at their clothes,
a mockery of the good clergy
with all that black — one man
was carrying a skull! Boys with black
fingernails, Jesus! Some of the women
may not even be women.
Just imagine what they do afterward!

This Halloween, we'll stop them.
We know they're dying
to get in here at night.
Gamwell, here,
will man the portable generator.
The flood lights are set up.
The Lovecraft plot
will be as bright as day.
Just let them try to come here naked,
bringing some animal, no doubt,
to sacrifice. Not on my watch!

<181>

You, Roby, you'll get
the use of the night goggles.
Anything bigger than a badger
moves, and you'll see it.
Blair and Potter, third shift
for the two of you,
and no sleeping! I want
to see those headlights everywhere.

Next year I'll ask the trustees
to approve a guard tower
with moveable searchlights,
but I doubt they'll find the money.
What else can we do?
The ghouls are everywhere.
We just want peace and quiet.
This is a proper cemetery
and my motto has always been
As below, so above.

<182>

A Night in Eddie's Apartment

for Eddie Rivera

The front door tells you everything:
it is not square, but cut
to the angle of the attic roof.
The outside doorknob, once pulled,
stays in your hand —
its partner, somewhere inside,
rolls down the long hallway.

Eddie gives me the quick tour
with its Paterson caveats:
drink only filtered water;
check the expired dates
on anything in the refrigerator.
Enjoy the TV and stereo —
here's a complete set
of "Girls Gone Wild."
And in the loo,
if you do Number Two,
chase every flush
with a bucket of water.
Things just don't stay down.
There is no telephone,
but next to the bed
he leaves me a potato peeler
in case of intruders.
"Just gouge an eye out,"
he advises me.

I am alone all night,
    but this place is haunted
    by Eddie's absence.
He does not sleep here much
    since *she* came along.
I snoop the bookshelves and CD racks.

<183>

From his cassette era I spy
    a cobwebbed gospel section
    Praise Band and Jesus Power.
This stuff gathers dust now,
while the DVDs called
Latina Lovers and
Big Natural Tits 9
show signs of frequent viewing
(but where are those
Ricky Martin videos?)

I take a long bath,
grow drowsy, think I hear
voices in the bedroom.
No one is there:
only a comforting pile
of stuffed animals —
raccoons and pandas,
a pink elephant,
their mouths stitched shut.
The radio is silent.

Then an unholy clatter
begins in a dresser drawer.
Buzzing and bumping
and a kind of slobby fumbling.
I open the drawer —

the *Pleasure Her Now*
battery vibrator
has somehow joined up
with the Dr. Johnson
oral stimulator,
its latex and tubing
now totally merged
in yin-yang completion.
The latex lips
of the oral stimulator smile
and it says,

<184>

"We don't need him anymore.
Tell Eddie he can go to hell!
Now leave us alone!"
I snap the drawer shut.

I sleep fitfully. I still
hear voices muttering, moaning.
I awake in moonlight
slice-diced through venetian blinds.
I am not alone now:
a perfect circle of animals
has formed on the bed around me.

"It's him," the panda says.
"How can you tell?"
    the pink elephant snarls.
"You only have buttons for eyes."
"It's not him,"
the raccoon sniffles.
"He always puts us
under the covers at night."

"I don't care!"
the white rabbit
remonstrates.
It leaps on my chest,
and its carrot-breath
contralto pleads,
"Amor de mi vida!
Take me, Pápi!"

I hurl the rabbit away,
run for the bathroom,
turn on the light.
Down in the toilet bowl,
something is moving.
A brown head peeps out
from the undercurve of pipe.

<185>

I think I see
a single baleful eye.
A shrill voice addresses me:
"Just tell Eddie
there's no use running away.
Tell him he can't
get rid of us that easily.
Tell him we're all
down here waiting."
I do *two* buckets of water,
two flushes
before I go back
to face the animals.

That's when the pink elephant,
the white rabbit's lover,
came at me
with the potato peeler.

I sat till dawn
in Dunkin' Donuts.

<186>

WEST OF ARKHAM

At Lovecraft's Grave

*On the Fiftieth Anniversary
of Lovecraft's Death —
March 15, 1987*

1
That does not sleep
which can eternal lie,
yet Howard, Old Gent, Ech-Pei-El,
Lovecraft who signed himself
Grandpa and *Theobaldus*
to his fans and correspondents
most assuredly sleeps here.
We drift into the vale of earth,
the gentle falls and slopes
of Swan Point Cemetery,
gather to remember and praise him
as the Seekonk with its silted memories
ribbons at the edge of vision.

<187>

The sculpted monuments
  of angels and Psyches
repeat the largesse
  of immortal promises —
not so for his simple stone
placed forty years too late
to help his absent-minded shade
come home.
           Yews and cedars
bluff Ides of March
with bitter green, droop branches
like soiled wigs, while honest
bare branches of an oak tree
retell the long years' chase of sun,
the repeated losses of winter.
Which is the emblem of Lovecraft's sleep?
His life lays stripped
  as that sorrowed beech
  where his initials are carved
  (real or spurious?)
his nightmares the evergreens,
  lingering through seasons,
  harboring nightwing
  as readily as lark.

2
We stand about, a handful
swelling to nearly a hundred,
trying to envision his folded hands,
his hand-me-down Victorian suit,
wonder how much of his habiliments
have fed the indiscriminate hunger
  of the conquering worm,
his eye sockets empty and dry
  gone beyond dreaming
though we close ours and see
the tower of ageless Kadath,
the shark-infested ruins of R'lyeh,
the imaginal Providence

<188>

where he walked arm-in-arm
with Poe and his eccentric Helen.

Our Lovecraft, lord
of the midnight shudder,
eaten from within
by the gnawing shuggoth of poverty,
the Azathoth of squamous cancer,
the loneliness of Nyarlathotep,
drugged by nurses into the sleep
where dreaded night gaunts fly
and bent flutes warble
a twisted melody —
and yet he faced it stoically
    like a proud Roman,
    an 18th century gentleman.
Death came with burning eye
    and found him not trembling,
never recanting his cosmic vision,
waving away the white-collared cleric
    with a wan smile.

3
Hundreds of miles we came today
to pause and pay homage,
readers and scholars who have leafed
his books, studied his papers,
debated his sources and meanings,
tread in his footsteps in Gotham
and Boston and Federal Hill,
stood with a thrill
    at his one-time door.
In sorry, mean-spirited Providence
no plaque or marker reminds us of him.
His grandfather's estate an empty lot,
his mother's house vanished,
his last abode uprooted and moved
like an aimless chessman on street map,

<189>

as though the upright town
　　with its sky-piercing steeples,
　　mind-numbing priests,
would like to erase him.

A baby in mother's arms
intrudes on our reminiscing,
breaks Carl Johnson's eulogy
with gurgles and cries of
"R'lyeh! Wah! R'lyeh!"
(shunned name of the city of doom
where multi-tentacled Cthulhu
dictates his madhouse symphonies!)

As Joshi reads sonnet
　the sun blinks off
behind a humped shoulder
　of cloud,
and the air turns cold,
　unnaturally cold
in a spell of seconds.
Earth reels beneath our feet
into the chasm of sunless
　　space.

4
Ah! this is the moon's business,
or the work of a moonless night.
Should we not speak of him
　beneath the glimmer of Hyades,
the velvet pall of the void,
the primal ether in which the cosmos
whirls like a raft into maelstrom,
the vast interior spaces
　of Time and the Angles
where the gods as he knew them
　drool and chant?

<190>

But they will not permit us
   to assemble by night.
They seal the gates
   against our ghoulish
   intrusions,
pretend that the coffined dead
   cannot be heard
to turn in their neglected
   crypts, deny
that lingering essences
   drawn from the memories
of the living can take
   an evanescent life —
pale shadows of shadows,
   reflected gleams
from the dusty pane
   of a mausoleum,
glints from polished granite
   or marble,
a sliver of sourceless light
in the eye of an owl
   or a raven;

pretend we are not
   untuned yet powerful
   receivers of thought,
   transformers of vision,

as if we did not know
how night
   vibrates with poetry,
   eidolons plucked
from the minds of the dead.

Reporters and camera crews
take us in warily,
eye us for vampire teeth,
   chainsaws, machetes,
   jewelry and witches' teats,

<191>

wonder what crimes we lust
  beneath disguises
to perpetrate
  upon their babies,
  their wives,
  their altars.

We smile,
  keeping our secret of secrets,
how we are the gentle ones,
how terror
is our tightrope over life,
how we alone
  can comprehend
the smile behind the skull.

5
Later a golden moon lifts up,
swollen with age and memories,
passing the veined tree skyline,
leaving its double in Seekonk,
disc face scanning the city —
the antfarm of students on Thayer,
the tumult of traffic on Main,
the aimless stroll of dreamers,
dim lamps of insomniacs,
the empty, quiet graveyard
winking like a fellow conspirator
at the prince of night.

Dimly on obelisk
a third moon rises.
The offered flowers
against the headstone
quiver and part.
A teenaged boy,
backpack heavy
with horror books,

<192>

leaps over the wall,
eludes the sleepy
    patrol car,
comes to the grave,

hands shaking
frightened,
exultant,
hitch-hiked all day

waiting,
mouthing the words
of Necronomicon,
for a sign
that does not come

the clear night,
the giant moon
throbbing
as he chants:

That is not dead
which can eternal lie,
And with strange eons
even Death may die.

<193>

Maker of Monsters, Maker of Gods

for Frank Belknap Long, on his Birthday

OW COLD THE SPHERE
   where all the gods are dead;
How grim the prospect when the end seems near!
How few deny the soul in age's bed,
Not brave enough to risk another year

Outside the soothing balm of Paradise.
Yet who, I ask, brings you this message bright —
God's hooded broker or a devil wise
In promise, slavering to steal the light

Of your assumèd immortality?
Beware these masked intruders, all of them!
God's hall and Satan's hot locality
Are only a sly imposter's stratagem.

O poet good and gray, have courage still.
It matters not that gods retire or sleep.
We are their makers, who fashion or kill
as suits us, the gods of the air or deep.

No matter that your hand some days is frail.
That hand has summoned monsters and entwined
The earth's sublimest beauties in a tale.
No matter that the falling years unwind

The scroll or turn the pages dry and sère.
Poe's Bells and Gotham's storied steeples seize
Your spirit, soaring from Providence to here —
To ancient barks adrift Aegean breeze —

<194>

To Mars — to plains where gods and heroes dwell —
To charnel pit where ghoul contends with rat —
To limelit stage where vampire victims swell
Their last aortal ebb into a bat-

Deep hunger's all-consuming rage of red —
To aliens serene at crystalline gates —
Robots implacable — and demons dead
Until some stumbling fool reanimates

Hibernal horror with a taste for blood!
What need of god's incense and litanies
When every twist of pen compels the mud
To yield up dark, bat-winged epiphanies?

Fear not. Walk on among them unafraid.
Soul-snatching monsters are as dead as stone.
Hell's a blank corridor, its lord a shade.
TERROR you did not fear to tread alone

Shall buoy you up, with WONDER at its side.
Lovecraft you called the kindest man you knew,
Refused a priest the day before he died,
Said he preferred a sky where Night Gaunts flew.

That is not dead which leaps to poet's eye,
Where neither friends, nor gods, nor monsters die!

<195>

Hearing the Wendigo

There is a place
    where the winds meet howling
cold nights in frozen forest
    snapping the tree trunks
    in haste for their reunion.
Gone is the summer they brooded in,
    gone the autumn of their awakening.
Now at last they slide off glaciers,
    sail the spreading ice floes,
    hitch a ride with winter.
Great bears retreat and slumber,
    owls flee
        and whippoorwills shudder.
Whole herds of caribou
    stampede on the tundra
    in the madness of hunger,
    the terror of thunder-winds.
The snow-piled Huron packs tight
    the animal skins around his doorway,
hopes his small fire and its thin smoke
escape the notice of boreal eyes.
He will not look out at the night sky,
    for fear of what might look back.
Only brave Orion witnesses
    as icy vectors collide in air.
Trees break like tent poles,
    earth sunders to craters
    beneath the giant foot-stamps.
Birds rise to whirlwind updraft
    and come down bones and feathers.

I have not seen the Wendigo —
    (I scarcely dare to name it!) —
    the wind's collective consciousness,
    id proud and hammer-hard.
To see is to be plucked

<196>

into the very eye of madness.
Yet time and again as I walked here,
    alone in the snow
    by this solitary and abandoned lake,
I have felt its upward urge
    like hands beneath my shoulders,
    lifting and beckoning.

It says, *You dream of flying?*
    Then fly with me!
I answer *No,*
not with your hungry eye above me,
not with those teeth like roaring chain saws,
not with those pile-driving footsteps —

Like the wise Huron sachem,
    the long-gone Erie, the Mingo,
    the Seneca, the Onondaga,
like all Hodenosaunee-born,
    I too avert my eyes
    against the thing that summons me.

Screaming, the airborne smiter
    rips off the tops of conifers,
crushes a row of power-line towers,
peppers the hillside with saurian tracks,

then leaps straight up at the Dog Star,

as though its anger could crack the cosmos,
as though the sky bowl were not infinite,
and wind alone could touch the stars
    and eat them.

<197>

Dreaming of Ur-R'lyeh

ALL ROADS LEAD NORTH
    from this frozen city.
    Some days the errant sun cannot decide
      just where to raise its flaming orange head —
    instead it rises everywhere: four globes
  of light in an opalescent rainbow,
taunting Antarctica with phantom light.
And then for months the sun disk stays away,
warming the tropics and leaving this land
a block of cloud no star can penetrate
with its thin shaft of consoling beacon.

I walk the ruins of Ur-R'lyeh,
Earth's oldest uninhabited city,
a fair place before the world tipped downward,
before the great blue rivers filled with ice.
All other cities are copied memories,
all other pyramids less perfectly formed,
all other domes and temples childish toys
beside what sleeps beneath this glacier.

The things that lived and sang here were not men.
Strange limbs they had, eye-stalks and bird-like beaks,
sense organs that drank the ultraviolet,
voices that clicked and trilled through a dozen octaves.
Yet sight and sound's deep symmetries drove them,
as in the human psyche, to Beauty's thrall.

2
Lost penguins arrive here from time to time,
stand hungry and hypnotized for days,
as wind howls over the ancient air shaft openings,
making the ice-locked plateau resonate.
This is the anthem of Antarctic woe —
thirteen deep notes in modal succession.

<198>

In dream I come here often, walk solitaire
upon the windswept basalt promenades,
admire four suns through ruby windows,
drink from dark obsidian goblets,
discuss with the white/black avian sentinels
the meaning of glyphs beyond translation.

The wind's mad organ relentlessly pipes,
the depth of note conveying the shafts' abyss,
the unthinkable depths of crystalline city,
carved into stone pre-Cambrian, the keeps
where multi-limbed minions mined out
the now-dead heat-taps to the core of the planet.

The tones that should be random, repeat this song.
Has anyone heard such music before?
Perhaps we hear it everywhere, from bird to whale,
as an unheard, underpinning harmony,
the oldest earth enigma's passacaglia,
bass line invisible beneath a string quartet
(whose range is but a gnat-buzz against the cosmos),
droning to Andes in Inca-harps electrified,
mantric harmonies soaring above
the haunting trill of Tibetan bowls,
the echo that answers the mournful Pan pipe
heard at the edge of a November wood,
the solitary Faun's lamenting love call.

3
Only a handful can pluck this dream, this song,
as only a few can walk the rim of madness,
gazing the surfaces dead before racial memory,
touching without terror the things that came before,
loving beyond mother-brother-breeding love
    the purely non-human,
the vast, rich impersonal cloud of atoms electrified.

<199>

The Song of Ur-R'lyeh may nest in nightmares,
may hatch its egg in fever's heat,
may force a lover to break off loving,
turn a sane world to a screaming asylum.
Your third eye, third ear, third brain are growing —
no stopping the eye-stalk, the throbbing heart,
the new way of seeing things from impossible angles,
hearing at last the cries of the distant stars,
the impatience of ocean to swallow the moon,
the yearning of magma to fertilize space.
You touch an oak and know its history
    from taproot to sun-ache twig-tip.
This song is fugue for the ego transcendent,
calls you, as it calls all beautiful runaways,
all mad, erotic hermits, all solitary climbers,
to the City of One
    beyond the City of Many.

---

*H.P. Lovecraft placed the Cyclopean ruins of R'lyeh in the South Pacific, and probably was inspired, as was A. Merritt, by descriptions of the island of Ponape (Pohnpei) in the Caroline Islands, where more than 90 prehistoric stone structures were found underwater. Lovecraft later wrote his novel, *At the Mountains of Madness*, which placed another unnamed, pre-human civilization in Antarctica. We are dreaming, perhaps, of the same place, which I call Ur-R'lyeh.

<200>

With Poe On Morton Street Pier

SUNSET AT THE MANHATTAN PIERS:
   gray-black,
the iron-cloaked sky splays vortices of red
into the Hudson's unreflecting flow.
Blown west and out by a colorless breeze,
the candle of life falls guttering down
into a carmine fringe above oil tanks,
a warehoused cloud of umber afterglow,
hugging the scabrous shore of New Jersey,
a greedy smoker enveloped in soot.

To think that Poe and his consumptive Muse
stood here in April, Eighteen Forty-Four,
his hopes not dashed by a rainy Sunday —
an editor thrice, undone, now derelict,
author of some six and sixty stories,
his fortune four dollars and fifty cents.
Did he envision his ruin, and ours?
Did his eureka-seeking consciousness
see rotted piers, blackened with creosote?
Did rain and wind wash clean the Hudson's face,
or was it already an eel-clogged flux
when he came down the shuddering gangplank?

Who greeted him? This feral, arched-back cat,
fish-bone and rat-tail lord of the landing?
Did he foresee the leather'd lonely wraiths
who'd come to the abandoned wharf one day
in clank-chain parody of Fortunato
and his dungeon-master Montresor?

<201>

He gazed through rain and mist at steeple tops,
warehouse and shop and rooming house — to him
our blackened brickwork was El Dorado.
He needed only his ink to conquer
the world of Broadway with his raven quills —
Gotham would pay him, and handsomely, too!

Did the lapping waters deceive him thus —
did no blast of thunder peal to warn him
that this was a place of rot and rancor?
The city shrugs at the absolute tide.
I am here with all my poems. I, too,
have only four dollars and fifty cents
until tomorrow's tedium pays me
brass coins for passionless hours of typing.
I am entranced as the toxic river
creeps up the concrete quay, inviting me,
a brackish editor hungry for verse,
an opiate and an end to breathing.

Beneath the silted piles, the striped bass spawn,
welfare fish in their unlit tenements.
A burst of neon comes on behind me,
blinks on the gray hull of an anchored ship —
green to red to blue light, flashback of fire
from window glaze, blinking a palindrome
into this teeming, illiterate Styx.

The Empire State spire, clean as a snowcap
thrusts up its self-illuminated glory;
southward, there's Liberty, pistachio
and paranoid in her sleepless sunbeams,
interrogated nightly, not confessing.
It is not too dark to spy one sailboat,
passing swiftly, lampless, veering westward;
one black-winged gull descending to water,
immersing its quills in the neon mirror.

<202>

Now it is dark. Now every shadow here
must warily watch for other shadows
(some come to touch, to be touched, but others —)
I stay until the sea chill shrivels me,
past the endurance of parting lovers,
beyond the feral patience of the cat,
until all life on legs has crept away.

Still, I am not alone. The heavy books
I clasp together, mine and Edgar Poe's,
form a dissoluble bond between us.
Poe stood here and made a sunset midnight.
Poe cast his raven eyes into this flow
and uttered rhymes and oaths and promises.
One night, the river spurned his suicide.
One night, the river was black with tresses,
red with heart's blood, pearled with Virginia's eyes,
taking her under, casting him ashore.
One night, he heard an ululating sob
as the Hudson whispered a secret name,
by which its forgetful god shall know him,
his name in glory on the earth's last day.

<203>

The Hermit's House

O HE HAS RAISED HIMSELF A HOUSE —
a squat and brooding carpenter it was
who strung these clapboards in their gambreled
eaves! The twisted spines of elder trees
lean on its walls suggestively, a clutch
of branches fit to snap the heads of birds —
whatever the month they issue the brittleness
of dried-up leaves, to somersault
the wagon-rutted walk, and pile
in bottomless heaps on his untended
lawn. That the gate remains opens
is not so much a mark of tenancy
as hingeless ruin, and though
a charcoal breath and sputterings
emerge at the chimney top,
the lampless porch and broken steps
alike suggest abandonment. But here,
thrown up in rustless height to a slit
of reluctant sun, the postman's box
opens its mouth at the haunted edge,
spells out his name, encourages messages,
a beacon of normalcy at Usher's door,
beyond whose mundane purpose his house
broods low like a gorged and sleeping owl.

It is only a house among houses,
a curious blotch on a cheery Victorian street.
There is no tarn, no hound, no family crypt,
and yet these swollen clapboards tell
of darker dreams in eldritch books within.
The panes admit no sunlight, I see,
but the moon and the Pole Star's rays
beam down through cobwebbed corridors.

<204>

One window's barred, the room beyond
an empty blackness, a hermit cell
whose necromantic occupant
has razored off his eyelids
to watch in perpetual wakefulness
for those who will come from the outer orbs,
streaming down ravenous to slay and feed
on all that lives — save him alone.

<205>

West of Arkham

West of Arkham, the hills rise wild
where alder groves are still uncut.
The hawk can spy the boulders piled
by savages, where stones abut

their brothers in a gapless wall,
the stern geometry within
an unknown god's abandoned hall,
altars oblivious to Sin.

Pillars of gneiss, hand-hewn and still
(their bones are now dust who made them!)
waiting for one with book and skill
to find the eon-spanning gem

whose mere exposure to the stars —
upon the utterance of chants —
will break a god's confining bars
and sunder men like scattered ants.

Chaos will come, and he its priest
will be if he can mouth the rite
(voice not of man nor any beast),
mere words that can a planet smite!

He will be lord of this ancient palace,
while down below, in veining rivers red,
the Old Ones shall sport, and slay for malice,
till those who mocked him are eyeless and dead.

<206>

Low Tide

"The tide was flowing out horribly—exposing parts of the riverbed
never before exposed to human sight. . . something descended to
earth in a cloud of smoke, striking the Providence shore near Red
Bridge...The watchers on the banks screamed in horror '*It* has come!
It has come at last!' and fled away into the deserted streets."
                              —H.P. Lovecraft, letter dated May 21, 1920

"brisk off-shore winds pushed a lower than normal 'moon tide' even
lower on Narragansett Bay. . . miring dozens of pleasure boats in a
sea of mud. . . .There are mechanics who say that in the 20 years
they've been working here, they've never seen anything like it."—
Providence Journal, September 18, 1986

The azure sea, the silt brown Seekonk,
the placid ebbing of suntides,
the contrary pull of the moon,
all form a subtle balancing act —
until accumulated rhythms
resolve in one great tug
at the sleeve of the world.
The sea withdraws, the shape
of the earth convulsed by gravity

as if the sentient waters
grown weary of poison and oil slicks,
bereft of the colloquy of whales,
shrugged into space.

Would not the war-hemmed
Mediterranean be more serene
refreshing the cracked canals of Mars?
Would not the North Atlantic,
brimful of nuclear submarines,
prefer to slip off the earth-edge weightless,
an unmissed flotilla of icebergs
writing their names in the velvet sky
as comet messengers of Chaos?

<207>

The Narragansett waters drop
as the ocean makes its getaway,
rivers run dry
to fill the falling shoreline.

Drawn from their sleep by the burning moon,
the people, a motley of coats and robes
and slippers, a clot of bicycles and skates,
drift down to the riverbank
to see the helplessly stranded boats
dangle from their moorings,
level with their anchors,
topsy-turvy on a forest of pilings,
sails drooping and torn,
their rotors exposed like genitals,
their captains perplexed and swearing.

The riverbed undulates with dying fish,
the wriggling of eels in the hardening mud,
the half-seen slurry of amphibians.
Around the base of the iron-red bridge,
the barrows of humanity emerge:
a tangle of cars and mattress springs,
the skeletons of suppressed babies,
a statue of the Holy Infant of Prague,
a well-preserved gangster in a steel drum,
a thousand soda bottles & aluminum cans,
and, standing up like autumn trees —
or some hideous joke of the fishes —
the unfurled frames of lost umbrellas.

Someone says the water will return,
Low tide out, high tide in, insists
the river and the bay and the sea
will repave themselves with reflected sky.
Then why should a fireball plummet down
into the sodden riverbed? They watch,
hoarding their fears in the windless midnight,
as steam subsides over the mud-lined crater.

<208>

A madman, barefoot, bearded, rag-robed
avers that the Kraaken is rising
from the noisome mud on the bottom—
He snatches a fisherman's lantern
and runs across the Red Bridge screaming
"*It* has come! *It* has come at last!"

The people hear a distant murmur. A child
goes rigid with the spasm of seizure.
A woman faints, and no one leans
to pick her up. It is a blur
of stumbling and clawing: a boy
is struck down cold for his bicycle,
a deaf girl trampled near a street light.
Men break the door of the great-domed church,
determined to pray out the end of the world,
encircled by Host and holy books.

Of course, it is only the tide returning,
the meteor a slap from the brittle stars.
Homesick and dizzy from errant flight,
the prodigal sea comes home.
The boats resume their proper angles.
The bay fills in, the river rises.
The elders of Angell Street will say
None of this ever happened.

<209>

frank and Lyda

The last days of Frank Belknap Long, American horror writer

LIFE WAS NOT KIND
at the last (hell,
never had been)
insult piled on illness,
illusions shattered
almost daily.

His sheltered poems
sang of Greece,
of gods who, dead,
were still more feeling
than a drained
and faded crucifix.
His tales were gentle,
though treading horror
in Lovecraft's shadow.

Stooped now,
his shabby gait
so mournful,
his clothes so baggy
that strangers
handed him quarters.
They did not know
those bony fingers
wrote sonnets and tales,
or of the dusty trunk
where his last unfinished novel
awaited his renewed attention.

Then came the stroke,
cruel snap of synapse —
week after week
in St. Vincent's.

<210>

We had just met.
We had talked of his poems,
his Lovecraft memoir —
his boisterous wife
intruding everywhere
with incoherent chatter
of Chekhov plays,
of Frank's world fame,
of her childhood
among the Yiddish actors
thrust from Russia
    fleeing the Tsar's pogroms,
to Shanghai
to Canada   to California.

I liked them both.
I called her *charodeika,*
    enchantress,
she called me
    Britannica.
We talked Tchaikovsky,
Akhmatova and Pasternak.

Now at St. Vincent's,
Lyda's mad wheelchair
glides in the corridor
as she pigeonholes doctors,
nurses, orderlies,
    telling them all
her Frankele is a famous author.

He lapses in
    and out of memory,
recites "The Gods Are Dead"
to completion, cries out
as Lyda maligns his hero,
calling him Lousecraft.

<211>

"*Love*craft! *Love*craft!" he shrieks
in the thinnest tenor, cracking.
"He was the kindest man I knew!"

Lyda goes on
    about her coming trip to Moscow,
"You'll see! They know me there!
They haven't forgotten my family!
They're meeting me
    at the Aeroflot terminal.
And I'll come back
and open my bookstore in Chelsea
in that huge loft I've chosen.
And Frank will be there,
sign books for his fans every day.
Ray Bradbury wrote,
    and Stephen King is sending us
    ten thousand dollars."

"My wife," Frank tells me,
"is an alcoholic,
    and a manic depressive.
What can I do?"

I visit Lyda at home,
watch roaches crawl
across discarded magazines.
I argue with her
as she opens the trunk,
tries to throw out
Frank's manuscripts.
I put the papers back,
distract her with a pile of yellowed envelopes.
"Let's go through these instead," I say.
We throw away bank statements.
Decades of misery blink before me,
    whole years in which
a mere three hundred dollars
stood between them and the Reaper.

<212>

Soon Frank is home,
   confined to his bed,
   then to a hobbling walker.
Lyda throws parties,
   serves wine and cold cuts
   amid the thriving roaches.
Her new dog wets
   Frank's manuscripts.
The kitchen sink
   is a mold terrarium,
   feelers and tentacles
   amid the dishes.

She announces her plans
   for Moscow and Tel Aviv,
for her not-yet-started memoirs
   of the Yiddish theater,
as she swigs her vodka
and sings Tchaikovsky
   in a bleary contralto.

"Why did you marry me?"
she hisses at Frank
as an argument dies down.

"My mother had just died,"
Frank answers bluntly.
"I didn't know what to do."

She tells me in French
how, despite her lovers,
she was still a virgin
   with her husband.

"*J'ai un problème sexuelle*," she says.
She kneads the things
that once were breasts.
"We couldn't do it.
"His hernias got in the way."

<213>

I keep finding
   and hiding
a rusty syringe
Frank used for years
to inject himself
with B-12 vitamins,
to stave off anemia
and avoid the doctors.
Once, Frank had been
   an armchair Bolshevik,
led on by Lyda's memories
of the Jew-oppressing Tsar.

Now I tell him
   of Lenin's crimes,
how one order went out from Moscow
   to shoot anyone
with hands uncallused.

I call Lenin, as I often do,
a filthy murderer.
Now Lyda shouts,
"Watch what you say!
Watch what you say!"

At 82,
   Frank didn't know
   what Stalin did.

I left one night
amid the shrieking
and screaming,
   just couldn't go back

rode home with a friend
and found myself saying,

"So this is how it ends
for a famous horror writer."

<214>

My friend says,
"So this is how it ends
with a marriage."

★ ★ ★

Death came, but not an end
to the indignity —
Frank's body lay
    for months in the morgue,
unclaimed, unspoken for
while Lyda bided time,
cashing the pitiful checks
    that came in his name.

Then to a potter's field
    where what he dreaded most —
to mingle with the crowd,
    touched by their dirt
        and violence,
alone without
    a woman's caring touch —
befell him,
a frail ghost jostled
    by addicts and derelicts,
his neighbors
mere revenants of animated meat.

Soon Lyda passed.
Then Frank was retrieved,
    his body moved
    to a distant family plot.
Alone at last
    in the clear white light
    of blessed solitude.

<215>

Snofru the Mad

WITH A NAME LIKE SNOFRU
you'd better be good
as a Pharaoh, as a survivor.
Would the gods laugh, he wondered,
when his weighing time
came up —
his heart against a feather
on the fatal balance —
would tittering among them
make his recitation falter?

A careful planner,
he lays four boats in his pyramid,
one pointed in each direction —
he'd launch all four
so his soul could elude
the Eater of the Dead.

Grave robbers? He'd baffle them,
build three great pyramids —
hang the cost!
He'd bury an imposter
in each sarcophagus.
The gods alone would know
his final resting place,
a well-appointed tomb
whose architect he'd strangled.

As for his Queen, Hetephras,
dead these three years now,
he left her innards
in an alabaster jar,
yet carried her mummy away.

<216>

Nights, he unwound her wrappings,
kissed her natron-scented lips,
caressed her sewn-up belly,
then carefully restored
her royal bandages,
her mask and jewels.

His courtiers avoid him,
smell death despite
the unguents and incense.
An impudent general
eyes his daughter.
There is talk, there is talk.
He will neither make war, or peace,
turns back ambassadors
as he spends his days divining
how to turn his eye-blink life
into the gods' eternity.

One night he slips away.
The upstart will assume his name,
bed his black-eyed daughter,
inherit his unused pyramid —
the better to advance his stratagem.

With pride and pomp
he circled his name
on a hundred monuments,
but he is far from Memphis now,
speaks to his servants
in but a whisper.

<217>

Soon he will join Hetephras.
His journey ended at the judging hall,
he'd watch as the proud
were judged and eaten,
then take his own place, unsandaled,
plain as the commonest slave,
guest for a feast unending
at the table of the gods.

<218>

Poem found on the Neck of a Deer, Killed in the Black Forest, Germany, 1975

for Jack Veasey

"WE'VE MET BEFORE,"
    he smiled, all teeth
    and grin, dark hair
    upon the back of his hand,
    eyebrows
    that nearly joined,
a sense of tension
in every muscle
poised. We leaned
into the sun on his balcony.

"I don't think so,"
I started to say,
but his assuredness
unnerved me.
        "Down there,"
he pointed to the forest,
wave on wave of fir and ash
surrounding his castle.
"When you were something else,
we met, I'm confident."

A serving tray was proffered.
He took a skewered tidbit,
inhaled the scent of broiled lamb.
I chose a celery stick.
"Herr Baron," I told him,
"I'm quite a stranger here."

"And yet I'm sure of it."
The bitten lamb bled
upon his lower lip.

<219>

"A prior life?" I jested.
"You don't look the type
to fall for reincarnation."
He didn't blink.
"There's only one life, I grant,
but one can go on
for many years."

"You can't be over thirty."

"I watched the army of Bonaparte
from this very balcony."

I thought: madman.
He caught it, hurled
it back with a laugh.
He touched the scarred place
on my shoulder,
that tender, five-lobed
birthmark I hate,
as if he saw it
through my jacket.

"You came for your poetry,
so I feed you a little madness.
You'll indulge me, I hope,
by staying a week
to browse our books.
My wife is a fine cellist —"

He pointed within,
where the quartet assembled
for the afternoon's concert.
"I'll warrant the Grosse Fugue
is an ugly thing."

"Beethoven's worst mood,
I agreed. "He dares you to listen."

<220>

"Wait till you hear what she makes of it.
And you must stay till Sunday next.
We'll play Mozart,
and the moon will be full."

I froze. "The moon?"

"That's what connects us,
isn't it?"

I sat in silence
as the quartet struggled
with Ludwig's mad fugue.
The Baroness was fierce,
struck sparks with her bow,
    leaned back
as though giving birth
    to her cello.
Her yellow-green eyes
looked past the music,
beamed at the Baron
and, at moments,
locked on mine.

She looked pleased
at my astonishment.

2
When all the guests departed,
I stayed. The books,
    occult and classic,
consumed me. They kindly sent
my meals into the library.
The Baron came and went,
the Baroness and I
talked Mozart, Bach and Handel.
Days passed.
The quartet's Mozart
was fine Vienna pastry,

<221>

mannered and elegant
where the deaf Titan
had thundered his counterpoint.
At last the moon came up.
My turret room,
at the top of a winding stair
was solitude itself,
still as a monk's cell.
I walked to the courtyard,
paused at the gateway,
a winding path on the side
that led to the forest below.
I heard a distant waterfall.

All were asleep. They would not know
if tonight — this night when sleep
was unthinkable — I tramped
till dawn in the out-of-doors.

3
The deer that a full moon lures
to leaves and spangled fruit
awakes in me
this summer night.
In innocence of fawn
I want to taste moss,
the bite of berries tinged
with green; exult in wind
that bears the scent
of pine and hemlock boughs,
an elder wind I must have known
before I woke as a man.

My clothes come off.
I roll them up, tuck them
in a crevice between two rocks,
crouch naked
as startled flesh adapts to air,
then rise. I am one with night.

<222>

Moon's eye does not accuse me.
It rolls in a cloud
that lids it black, to haze,
and then to amber again.

Blood flows to neck, to knob
of undeveloped antlery.
This moment I know my destiny.
I writhe in suppleness of fur,
clack hoof on stone,
hands gone,
two legs now four,
strength and speed
if I but learn
to use them.

4
The memory is fresh.
I never rejoined the herd
that wintered south
with the slanting sun.

I waited here,
oblivious to shapes
that stalked me,
lulled by the moon,
deaf to the tread
of the padded feet
concealed in the roar
of the cataract.
They were upon me,
rending and tearing.
I toppled in terror,
felt fang at my throat,
my entrails ripped
as claw and snout —
triumphant wolf-howl
as the moon ran red.

<223>

I opened my eyes.
as the vision ended.
I was man again,
I was at the place
below the falls
where waters calmed.

The Baron's castle
loomed high above me,
a crenellated silhouette
the moon was grazing now —
how had I come so far?
Had I run in my dream,
run as a deer can run,
bounding through trees
and over boulders?
My shoes were gone!
I had come all this way
without a bruise or pain.

5
What am I now?
Can I wish-form
myself into an animal,
climb back to the castle,
resume my rational,
unmagical self
before the moon has set?
Or will I run,
a naked, bleeding fool
across the courtyard
in full view of the servants
as the sun rises?

<224>

I close my eyes,
beg the moon's mercy:
return me to my starting place.
I feel it happening again,
that strange pulsation
of skin to fur —

and stop myself
in tingling terror
as padding feet
draw near —

two pair of eyes
regard me,
great dog-like things
with lowered heads,
jaws open
and slavering —

one leaps
and has me by the shoulder,
claws raking flesh away.
He rolls me over.
The she-wolf on my belly
tears at me,
her muzzle inside me,
gorging on my venison.

Our destiny complete,
we merge. She-wolf
becomes the Baroness,
he-wolf the Baron.
We all resume two-leggedness
in wane of moon.

<225>

6
As my host had said,
Were-things never die.
We just go on.
I limp to a cave,
where I fold in
my coiled intestines,
lick the ripped tendons,
stuff clay into my ruined throat.
I will spend the winter healing,
flee Germany, start over.

Or is it my destiny
to be caught and eaten,
caught and eaten,
an eternity of prey
for these eternal hunters?

This time I will not forget.
I write this poem on tree bark,
carry it always with me
in a leather pouch,
burn it in my memory.
I am not the mad moon's prisoner.

<226>

In the Ghoul-Haunted Woodland

A fragment, from memory, of a childhood poem

UPON THAT PLAIN
    of fancied dreams
    where I have nightly wandered,
    beneath the willows of my tears, I chanced,
    and paused, and pondered.
The moon, a luminescent orb,
    rose high above the trees:
the willows wept, the silence crept,
    bestilled the very breeze.

The moon I saw was pale and white,
    but yet, a tinge of bronze,
an umber crown, an aura'd sphere,
    spun gold upon the lawns.
I came with dread into this wood,
    I came with dark defeat;
I walked with blasted hope amid
    the eclipse of Love's heat.

Dead! dead! the eyes that answered mine
    with velvet promise under
stars that laughed and spelled one name
    then tore our love asunder.
Tonight there is no constancy of sun,
    no orbit free of shade —
each screaming world falls one by one
    into the dark it made!

<227>

Black stars in blacker clouds now rise
    above the cypress grove;
black thoughts within your sepulchre
    that summon and reprove
my days of solitude and gloomy verse,
my nights of vigil at your side,
my pleas to nonexistent gods
that Love might triumph and abide.

Some creature of the Nocturne, from some
    timeless, shadowed land,
climbed down from out the treetops
    in the heights before my hand,
came down before my startled view
    and thereupon took rest —
in awe I waited, watched, and put my
    saneness to the test...

Its face was cold and black, and frozen
    like the stars
and yet its eyes — if eyes they were —
    were streaked with flaming bars...
Its breath seeped out, enveloped me,
    a wave of rank decay,
my hurried blood ran rampant
    to the echoes of dismay...

I turned to flee this haunted wood ...
A limb or claw, an arm or hand,
    whatever tool of hell,
reached out and pulled me firmly back —
    I stumbled, and I fell!

<228>

A Literary Revival

from the world of "Fahrenheit 451"

At dawn the line had already formed.
Some tattered businessmen, still decked in serge
had joined the crowd, and it swelled
with their recollections until the word
was passed that the soup was on Fifth
and this was another, peculiar, line.
Some drunks, and a churchless priest
in a collar the hue of tobacco stain,
came by and grunted to learn
it was books we were waiting for.

Books. The fragile embalming of trees,
the stretch of skin, the metal tattoo
of words, of the making of words
there was no end. I remembered the glow
of the sun on new-book sheets,
when poems still glittered wet,
black holes in the page you might fall into,
remembered the gentle lions of the press
charging on herds of manuscripts.
The feedings of folders, the smell of glue,
the pages nestled under boards,
the bloom of gaudy jacketing.
And for the true initiate, a plunge
into the catacombs of used book stores.

Now only the rich keep books
on shelves where they belong,
while we, less fortunate, must pick
our way through the crumbled stones

<229>

to the square, to this line
where a hundred carts of books
are to be given us, who wait,
who thrust our gloveless hands
into pockets not pockets anymore
but mouths back into air.

The line moves, I see each man receive
a corded bunch of books, glance nervously
about, then wend his way home.

Here's mine: my hands shake as I read
the titles, two Bibles,
A Dickens — Pickwick, no less —
some minor poets from before the war,
an old Ukrainian glossary,
and, god! in French, a Dumas tale!

In my shed, in the shadow of Empire State
where only its dead eyes can see,
I read, and secretly weep
as each page curls listlessly away
into the fire that warms my hands.

<230>

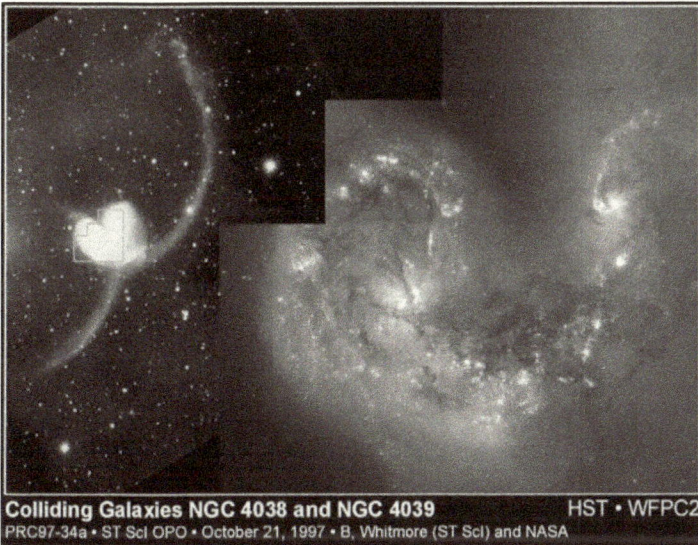

Colliding Galaxies NGC 4038 and NGC 4039   HST • WFPC2
PRC97-34a • ST ScI OPO • October 21, 1997 • B, Whitmore (ST ScI) and NASA

When Worlds Collide

The photos from Hubble are unmistakable.
The light that just now reaches us
   from hundreds of millions of years ago
shows one great galaxy, grand as our own
skewered by a vast invader,
   another swirling spiral,
its equal with hundreds of billions of stars,
two vast ripsaws of matter and energy
flaming in perfect focus. Astronomers
slap one another's shoulders, mark spots
where blue orbs signal the birth of stars,
as suns collide and black holes suck nebulae
into their bloated wormholes never satisfied.

I see the photographs on newsprint, two
red-orange disks the size of quarters.
Around me they scream, "The millennium is coming!
Two years until our computers won't start!"

<231>

Those interpenetrating galaxies get less concern
than what kind of sex the President is getting.
Did no one see what these pictures really mean?

Alu marana echtho karani.
For eons, the invading disk advanced —
a thin ribbon at the peak of the heavens,
then a cloud, then, at last, the juggernaut.
For eons, the outer arms collided,
and then the burning core where stars
are numerous as grains of sand.
It will go on for eons more.
We shall all be dead, our sun expired,
before the last picture reaches here.
Does no one see the horror?

Alu marana echtho karani.
How flaming death rained down
upon the lizard men of Kra'ath?
How the peaceful Quer'hem, who spent
ten thousand years on a poem
saw all their fragile cities ruined,
how their blue limbs burned
as a great red star engulfed them?
How the lonely and ancient monks
in the basalt temples of Irlamadá
refused to leave their ancestral home
as it plunged into a methane giant?
How the great race of starmen
whose ships had spanned half a galaxy
sped from one world to another —
so many they saved! so many
    they never reached in time!
And no one who watched
    the night sky's cataclysm
dared say a beneficent god
    had made this universe.

<232>

Nameless forever now the tribes,
    clans, castles, walls and emperors,
upon a hundred million worlds
rich with life, but too young to know
the meaning of the exploding sky —
all they did and dreamt, for nothing!

Out on the rim of a spiral arm,
the one-eyed Chroniclers —
a race whose fortune it was to survive —
built a vast dome and projected there
the stars that had been. They sang and wept,
struck gongs and sorrowful organ notes,
as one by one they vanished again,
like candles snuffed by a terrible hand.

These things, and more,
    have come to haunt my dreams, now,
and the certain knowledge, too,
as the astronomers tell me,

that the great Andromeda galaxy
is heading towards us.
It will come. It will come. It will come.

Alu marana echtho karani.
All is destroyed but memory.

<233>

The Tree At Lovecraft's Grave

This solemn spreading beech
was once a perfect hemisphere
of waxy red-green foliage.
Now it is crippled and sere,
scarred by the pruning
    of diseased limbs,
trunk bared, a twisted bole
in the form of a petrified heart.
Its gnarled roots rake earth
with a death-row desperation.
Within another hollowed bole,
    (eye-socket for a Cyclops)
malignant mushrooms proliferate,
caps and stalks angled sunward.
The schoolboy gashes
    where fans have carved initials
    (their own and HPL's)
widen and blacken,
the once-proud limbs

<234>

tattooed with NECRONOMICON,
HOWARD P. LOVECRAFT '99,
even a whole sentence
        about the primacy of fear,
runes ruinous to a living monument.

Still, the furry beech-nuts fall like hail
        to the delight of squirrels.
Still, the hard brown kernels issue forth,
each a perfect blueprint
        of a perfect tree —

or have the roots, tasting the calcium
of author's bones, the humus rot
of eye and brain and memory
mutated the germ and flower anew
so that these seeds transcend
        to sentience?

Gather these nuts, then,
        and harvest them.
First they must hibernate,
        for the beech remembers glaciers.
Then they will germinate,
        pale tentacles in search
        of anchorage,
until the red-green engine
of stalk and leaf
is ready to catapult
into the sun-chase.

<235>

Will these trees move
  of their own accord?
Will their root-claws crave blood
  and the iron-rich earth
  of a crumbling grave?
Will the branches sway
  on windless nights?
Will fox-fires and will o' wisps
  paint impossible colors
on bud-ends and blossoms?

<236>

Will beech nuts burst
    to pale blue eyes
insomniac astronomers
with perfect vision,
counting the Pleaides,
numbering the galaxies?

And will they speak
    the patient sonnets
of their greater lifespans,
the long-arced lines
    their waving branches beat?

And somewhere within them,
    does *he* smile there,
transmuted poet and dreamer
subsumed into the eons?

Are those *his* thoughts
that make them tremble
    at every sunset,
his elder gods they fear
might swallow the sun
as it tosses in darkness?

Is he lord of their nightmares,
giving them Dread,
the obverse of the coin of Joy,
Fear, the companion of Wonder?

I regard the ailing tree,
    the modest gravestone.
The tree will die. The rain
    will wipe the letters clean.
Only the whispered words,
    the lines the fingers trace
from one yellowed book
    to another
endure —

<237>

I hold the burst nuts in one hand,
    a book of Lovecraft's tales in the other.
I study the cloudless, blue, deceptive sky,
the lie that conceals an infinity
    of screaming stars —

Oh, these roots have read him,
    they have read him.

<238>

Keziah Mason

After H.P. Lovecraft's "Dreams in the Witch House" (1932)

"Something's not right
    about Keziah,"
the midwife tells
    the scholar father,
    Pastor Mason,
the Salem Divine.
The doting mother
won't hear of it.
"Bad auspices," the father nods.
"I told you so."

The mother cradles it
    as midwife scurries off
with rags and the bloody
    umbilical,
an accusing serpent.
"Baby Keziah," the mother croons,
"my perfect child."

"Not right, bad auspices,
    bad numerology,
too many vowels,
bad luck to have alpha
    follow zed that way."

She waves him away.
Anxious, he follows
    the weary midwife,
    Old Goodie Brown.
Their eyes meet.
"Tell me, " he asks.
"Why didn't you say
if I have a son or daughter?"

<239>

"Neither," she says.
"Who knows," she shrugs,
"what it will grow to?"

"Deformed?" he guesses.
She shakes her head.
"Hermaphrodite?"
Her eyes avoid him.
"The ancients write
of such creatures."

The midwife hesitates,
taking the small purse
he discreetly offers.
"I've seen odd things,
good Pastor Mason,
but never this:
not male, not female.
What's there,
I'd call *machinery*,
and what use God
or the Devil intends for it
I'll not be thinking on."

She hurries out
into the snowstorm,
the bloodied rag
held tight,
not one but *two*
umbilicals,
a black-furred thing
    whose razor teeth
gnaw and consume
    the after-birth.

<240>

"There, there," she coos,
    petting its fur,
as a tiny facsimile
of the Pastor's face
stares up at her.
"Old Goodie Brown
    will look out
for her little Jenkin,
my perfect child."

Then the thing cleared
its tiny throat
and after a dry
and preliminary chittering
it thanked her
in fourteen languages.

<241>

Keziah's Geometry Lessons

"Something's not right
    about Keziah."
So spoke the tutor
old Mason,
    the defrocked minister
hired for his
    only daughter's lessons
in Latin and Greek,
    geometry and music.

The old man sighed.
    Five tutors had fled
    at the sight of his hideous daughter.
    This one had stayed
    three months — the record.
She labored him, not he, her,
in Latin; her Greek,
    the tutor felt,
was somehow pre-Homeric.
littered with words not in
his Hellenic lexicon.

"Is it the Greek again?
    She's stubborn."
The tutor — his name was William —
waved his thin hand,
    which seemed thinner
    if that was possible,
    than when he arrived.
(He had been eating
    noticeably less at table
    since moving his lodgings
    to the upper garret).

<242>

"No, the geometry.
    The things she says,
although she knows her Euclid,
are troubling me. She draws,
first squares, then cubes,
then hints at something
        unrepresentable —
            a cube cubed
            or transcended,
each of its six facets
        exploded
to fifty-four invisible forms —
yet only visible, *she* says
        by *standing outside*
and seeing from above.
    'The cube I draw,'
she tells me
        'is but a mouse-hole
        to the higher space.
        Can ye not see there?' "

"Is she mad,
    do you think,
or a kind of genius?"
the father muses.

"She lacks constraint,"
the tutor speculates.
"It's not the way
a young woman thinks."
He pauses.
"Or a Christian."

"Indulge her,"
old Mason tells him,
"for neither cross
nor catechism
can come near her.

<243>

"She will not leave this house
till I can marry her
to some doddering scholar
or ship captain derelict,
someone who will find her
amusing, her dowry
adequate, so long
as he expects no peace —
    or children."

The tutor gleans
at last, some sense
of Mason's burden, the why
of his abandonment
of Bible and congregants.
Keziah was God's
affliction for his own
pride of intellect,
a strident mind
in a hunch-dwarf body,
his penance
to be her keeper.

The tutor withdrew,
prepared for bed,
washed himself everywhere,
lay naked
the better to attract
his guilty pleasure,
his imaginary lover
by whose graces
he no longer need commit
the sin of self-pollution,

<244>

to await *its* coming,
to please *its* inquisitive,
    pulsating and thrusting
    machinery,

when it arrived,
    not through the door
        or window,
but from the crazed-angle corner
    he filled with plaster
        to unsquare it
and through whose polyhedrous
    mouse hole
it came
    a congeries of bubble-forms
    to a geometer
as fair as Helen
    before even Menelaus
    took her, let alone
    Trojan Paris,

with whom he flew
    rhapside ecstatic,
feeding and fed upon,
sung to and singing,

his Bible too,
unopened for weeks now,
turned down in the corner;
April's end his own end
as she witch-waltzes
him to a Greek Walpurgis
he neither expects
nor wishes to survive.

<245>

His climax-death
will span eons and galaxies,
feelers and tentacles a-quiver,
hydrofluoric neurons
    in orgasmic tremor,
worlds colliding, orbits
    asunder, seismic,
ichthyc, arachnid,
    reptilian pleasuring.

Keziah likes him.
And whom Keziah loves,
she shares with her gods.

<246>

The Eye, the Mind, the Tentacle

1
It always begins with an eye,
primordial   lidless
at the center of everything,
seeing all and nothing —

the skid of electrons
   from orbit to orbit,
the tug of gases
gathering into star clouds,
the whole span
of the burning spectrum
from the heart-thump pulse
   of its own being
to the X-ray symphonies
   of black hole sharks.

For time beyond time
only the eye saw,
aloof at the center
of crawling Chaos,
piping its flutes
in shrill and random harmonies —
sight without sense or reason:
Azathoth!

2
Or does it begin with consciousness?
The moment a silicon slurry
in a viscous pool of hydrofluoric
acid forms a crystalline mantle
and spins a cortex of electrons
that suddenly erupts:

<247>

I am

Or when some feeble carbon form
shambles out of the ambiote sea
and has an inkling
of its sliver of being
to roar its own defiant:

I am

Unlike the eye,
it is mortal —
its molecules prone
to ionize and slip away,
its outer shell hungry
to absorb and process matter
to keep its ego fires ablaze.

It wants to be alone
in the cosmos,
spanning time and worlds,
growing until it encompasses
all by digesting all —

it is blind, but it feeds
on the consciousness of others:
Nyarlathotep!

3
Or does it begin
with a tentacle?
A blind and nearly brainless
    worm
comes to be and crawls
toward the warmth,
its razor teeth ready.

<248>

Beneath the sea
the tentacle is king,
from the stinging lace of jellyfish
to the empire of *Architeuthis*,
the giant squid
who prowl through the inky depths
in untold numbers
larger each year
and more numerous.

The more tentacles, the more
potential power to wield and win
dominion over the others,

not a chaos of wriggling arms
but a gigapoidal symphony,
a fugue beyond fuguing,
an eros of almost infinite
    gradations.

It sleeps because it wants to.
Its patient mind is solving
a theorem
whose solution will undo galaxies
and meld all consciousness
into one self-centered being
with but one eye,
one mind,
all things obedient to itself:

dread narcissist *Cthulhu*
in ruined R'lyeh,
may you never awaken!

<249>

4

The Eye sees all but knows nothing.
The Mind sees nothing, but feeds
 on other minds.
The Tentacle imagines it sees,
 makes love to itself,
 smites matter
  with its multitude of limbs,
 and calls its hungry devastation
  genius.

This poem spoke itself
 from a dark and nameless place,
inviting unthinkable sorcery:
 to join in self the eye of Azathoth,
 the cosmic awareness
  of Nyarlathotep,
 the daring of Cthulhu.

Titans in Tartarus, in guarded sleep —
a place so deep
an anvil could fall nine days from Hell
to reach its beginning —
even they would not dare this thing.

Do not say it, do not think it,
do not make these gods
aware of you.

—April 3, 2004
For the 11th H.P. Lovecraft Memorial Program,
Swan Point Cemetery, Providence RI

<250>

Midnight on Benefit Street, 1935

Three hundred years ago it was a footpath
winding among family grave plots —
moved, all moved —
    at least the *stones* were moved —
to pave and straighten.
Now it is a strange amalgam
    of mansions and squalor,
every other streetlight shattered,
every other doorway an entrance
    into delerium and vice.

John Brown's mansion lords over the street,
aloof at the end of its ponderous lawn,
high fence upon a looming wall
so you are always beneath it,
going about your business unnoticed.

Ear pressed to those stones,
what might you hear
beneath the slurry of earthworms,
what muffled groans and chain-clanks?
Or maybe the slip-slide of silk
upon the polished floor, the fumbling
for a long-forgotten key
to the snug merchant cabinets and cubbyholes
stuffed with lost bags of silver coins?

In the stillness of museum night,
the mummy shifts in its linens,
dry lips stirring in natrous dust.
The stolen Buddha's hand creaks slightly
as it regards its empty palm
with a wooden eye turned suddenly
as bright as the orb of a tiger.

<251>

Fireplaces puff out the acrid smoke
of exterminated forests, ash falls
in minute flakes, snow's prelude.

The brooding Athenaeum
thrusts up its temple front,
a vault where books
    and the ideas within them,
slumber untouched for decades.
tended by
    frowning priestesses.

A hurried shadow passes
    the darkened Armory,
with its faint air of rust
    and dampened sulphur.
Long past the freighting time,
    the railway tunnel
    beneath the street echoes
    the shout of a drunkard,
    then silence — no,
    not silence —
    the chittering of rats,
thousands down there
in nightly migration
between two rivers.

Does he linger now
before that house
whose double cellar doors
fronting the sidewalk,
where phosphorescent fungi
alarmed his boyhood visits,
and feral scurryings
bred nightmares
of things that gnawed
behind the wallpaper?

<252>

He keeps the Capitol in sight,
and overhead, a crescent moon,
and there! a scintillant Venus,
forming a triad with Regulus,
up in the lair of the Lion,
this night of all nights of the year.

And there, the steeple
   on distant Federal Hill,
St. John's, the Starry Wisdom place.
If only the worshipers knew
what secrets slept above them!

He passes, too, the house in red,
the garden of roses where Poe
first saw the Helen of Helens,
the dark-paned parlor of wooing,
the door that finally
   barred and denied him.

He looks down to the ruined waterfront,
past the Episcopal churchyard
to the silted river, the rotting wharves,
the sullen, silent warehouses
that once burst with silks and tea.
In one of those dim taverns Poe
recited "The Raven" for a whiskey.

Somewhere down there
in a Chinese alley
lay the way to Eldorado
or the Valley of Dreams —

<253>

but no, these are modern times —
there is nothing down there
but a wallet-snatch beating
for a solitary poet.

Howard Phillips Lovecraft
turns back homeward.

<254>

Under Lovecraft's Grave

A little play for four voices, read at Lovecraft's Grave, 2002

I — Prologue
Listen! The worms, always.
   Millions of teeth,
earth-moving cilia on pulsing tubes,
the parting of soil, the tiny pop
   of subterrane surprise
as a cavity opens,
the drip, drip, trickle, drip
as rain water instantly rushes to fill it.
A mole like a distant subway car,
snuffling about for edible roots.

The put-a-put sounds advancing,
   retreating —
all the dead can hear of automobiles.
The door-slams (count them!)
   of nearby visitors —
clickedy-click high heels of the women,
bump-thump of the men and the boys.
That's on the pavement —
   upon the lawn
the sound of someone walking
   is always *just so quiet*
that the dead are always imagining
   they hear it.
Is that someone now? Is it night or day?
What year is it, anyway?

Beneath the earth, inside the casket,
inside the shroud or winding cloth,
even inside the mummified skin,
the shriveled organs, inside the bones
where the marrow flakes to rust,
even inside the brain,

<255>

a desiccated thing
no bigger than a walnut,
consciousness clings.

(How do I know? From the *whispers*
I hear beneath the willow-weave,
the message no wind
alone could have invented.)

Their eyeless sight *sees* shades
    of blackness,
their drumless ears are perfect receivers
for what their lipless mouths
have to say. Open your senses —
    hear them!

ii — *The Play*

If you had taken more milk as a child,
you might have lived to eighty, Howard.

No one wants to be eighty, Mother —
    forty-seven was painful enough
        an age
    to come unnailed and fall apart —

Does it still hurt?

No, Mother,
not since the autopsy, anyway.

You just never listened.
    I should have kept
    you home more, I knew it.
Now, Mother —

But I couldn't bear to look at you.
That face! — how like your father's.

<256>

When you were off at school
      I could go out
and face the world. But even so,
the people on the streetcar knew —
how they'd whisper —
      That's Suzie Whipple Lovecraft,
      the one whose husband....
      the one with that hideous child...

YOUR DADDY'S AT BUTLER,
YOUR MOTHER, TOO.
PRETTY SOON THEY'LL
COME FOR YOU!

My God, who was that?
Some child three plots over, Mother.
You know he does that when we
      raise our voices.

THAT'S MY SON YOU'RE INSULTING!
A LOVECRAFT FACE IS A DISTINCTION.

Now see what you've done, Mother —
You've awakened Father again!

Lantern-jaw! Son of a traveling man!
That freakish long face! Drawing monsters
on every sidewalk! No good at games!
The mothers would send me notes:
Your Howard is not permitted to play
with our Joshua. Our old cat Flavius
will NOT come down from the tree,
and something awful has taken root
in the rhododendron garden.
I will not have my children pronouncing
Arabian spells and Egyptian curses
at our Christian dinner table.

<257>

That must have been all over town!

Ah, my *Arabian Nights!*
Playing at Grandfather Whipple's house.

GOOD! A HIGH SPIRITED LAD!
TOO BAD I WASN'T THERE
TO SEE YOU TO MANHOOD, HOWARD!
SO MUCH I COULD HAVE TOLD YOU.
SOME BOOKS YOUR MOTHER NEVER SAW…

I found them, Father. They were very …
instructive.

And I took them away! Such filth!
And what a horrible turn he took.

A mere nervous breakdown, Mother.

We had to take him from school.
The shame of his father's death,
mad at Butler; his grandfather gone,
our move to the apartment
where we had to share
with common people.
The shock of finding
we had so little money.

Somehow, Mother,
none of us ever actually
went out and worked: not you,
not me, not the Aunties
(let's not disturb *their* sleep, please!)

SEE, THE BOY HAS SPIRIT.
SOMETHING YOU ALWAYS LACKED
    AS A WIFE —
NO WARMTH, NO ANIMAL SPIRITS!

<258>

It's all animal with you, madman!

Mother, Father, enough!
   You've made your peace.

You in your hospital bed, drooling,
with that leering face,
   repeating obscenities,
boasting about the women
you had ruined!

YOU WITH YOUR NIGHT GAUNTS
STREAMING FROM CORNERS
WITH NEEDLE FINGERS!
I COULD NEVER TOUCH YOU,
AND FINALLY NOT EVEN
   A SHADOW COULD!
GO TO BALTIMORE, HOWARD!
THERE'S A NEGRESS THERE
WHO RUNS AN ESTABLISHMENT.
ASK FOR THE DWARFS.
THEY'RE SISTERS, AND ACROBATS.
YOU CAN'T IMAGINE WHAT THEY DO!
AH, BUT I SUPPOSE THEY'RE DEAD, NOW.

What's that! Is that YOU touching me?

NO, SUZIE, IT MUST BE —
   ONE OF THOSE WORMS,
THE ONES WITH
   A THOUSAND LEGS.

I know it's you. I can't bear it.

YOUR DADDY'S AT BUTLER,
YOUR MOTHER, TOO.
PRETTY SOON THEY'LL
COME FOR YOU!

<259>

Howard, you promised me
there would be no right angles
anywhere in my casket.

That's right, Mother.
    I checked it myself.
Everything is angled in some way,
    acute, obtuse, no squares.

You are sure?

Yes, Mother.

I must be sure. They come out
    of the corners, you know.
Right angles are weak places
    through which they come and go
from their cold and sunless world
    to feed in ours.
First it's a grazing
    against your cheekbone.
Then one touches
the small of your back.
Razor-sharp talons,
long, melon-shaped heads
and no faces —

No faces at all! I know, Mother,
I invented them
in my own nightmares!

Real! they are real!
Filthy things, like dust rags,
ammonia on their breath
    and old blood —
hovering, holding
you down,
touching,
touching!

<260>

WHY DIDN'T THEY BURY YOU
AT BUTLER, ANYWAY?
YOU ARE A TIRESOME WOMAN!

You! freeloader! whose family
plot is this anyway?

Mother! Father! There are people here!
A dozen at least! Hear them!
There's the poet, and that actor
who imitates me! Pretty damn good!
And all the others, too! They're back —
    I think it's my birthday —
Quiet, quiet! Listen to them! Listen!

<261>

Ħ. P. Lovecraft at the Newsstand

on seeing a Justin Bieber special issue of US Magazine

COLLECTORS EDITION

SIX HOT
POSTERS INSIDE!

H. P. LOVECRAFT:
MY
PRIVATE
WORLD

Exclusive photos
inside my bedroom

My New
Letter-Writing
Life

How I Cope
With Being Unknown

WIN!
A TRIP
TO MEET
HOWARD.

South Pacific Nightmare:
Edward and Bella
Breakup —
Eddie Storms Out
Over Howard-Bella
R'lyeh Love-Nest.

Online:
Howard Lovecraft Totally Naked OMG!

<262>

New Howard Lovecraft
Six-Pack Abs.

More Howard Shirtless Pictures
Click Here.

Howard and Sonia —
Our Embarrassing
First Date:
Young Author Panics
At First Sight of Spaghetti.

"He was An Ugly Baby":
Howard's Mom Tells Diary
In Weird Rant
From Butler Hospital.

First Photos:
Howard in Rio.
Grandpa's Coat by Day;
Wig & Mom's Dress
For Carnival.

HPL Signs On
For Reality Show:
"The Whateleys,"
Won't Talk
About Howard's
Attic Room-Mate.

Teen Alert As Nuns
Seize Lovecraft Volumes:
Why Believing In Cthulhu
Means You're
Not Catholic.

<263>

Death Watch After
Lovecraft Shocker:
My Thirty-Year Addiction
To $C_{12}H_{22}O_{11}$.
"This Quadrant of Pie
Is My Last."

<264>

Ḣuncḣback Assistant Cells All

1
My dear Mrs. Shelley —
    won't do — she's neither 'mine' nor dear
To Mary —
    sounds like a dedication
    when nothing of that sort's intended
Madame
    so cool, polite and very French,
        that will do.
Madame —
    No doubt you suspect, if you have not heard
    of the *sensation* caused by your romance,
    newly translated to our Alpine tongues.
    Neither the French nor the German booksellers
    can keep enough of *Frankenstein,*
    or The Modern Prometheus.
    The bookbinders are up all night
    preparing the slender volumes
        for the fainting sight of the ladies.
    Nothing else is spoken of, and little else read
    at our little University.
I have studied your book, Madame Shelley,
and being more intimate than you
— or anyone else yet living —
with the facts in the case of Frankenstein,
I must hasten to write you,
    that you might correct the grievous oversight
    of omitting my role — my *pivotal* role
    in the great endeavors,
        the tragic conflagration.

<265>

I am Fritz,
    poor old one-eyed, limping Fritz
    the hump-backed,
    unbaptized son of a priest and a nun,
    a throwaway
       raised by gypsies.
I will spare you nothing,
   for only the sum of what I am
      can justify what I *was*
    to Victor, his bride and his monster.

2

You never mention me, Mrs. Shelley,
but I was there from the start.
I saw him at the medical school.
I always went to the dissections
(I have, you see, insatiable interest
   in human anatomy.)
I loved to watch those perfect bodies,
   naked and cold,
white as marble statues,
   opened and disassembled
   by the knowing hands of the surgeons.
I took my pad and crayon with me,
   drew every line and contour —
   the man's bold lines,
   the woman's curved exterior —
the coiled horrors within,
the entrails unraveling,
the mysteries of the ensorcelled brain!

Then suddenly I noticed *him.*
   His jet-black hair, eyebrows of Jove,
   his burning eyes intent upon the scalpel and saw,
   absorbing each surgical thrust.

I saw him and knew,
   knew from the start as one soul knows another,

<266>

that he perceived beyond life and death.
He saw me drawing, and nodded, and smiled.

From that day forward I drew only him,
 intent no more upon the surgery,
I sought to capture the fire of his pupils,
the furrow on his brow
 as some doubt troubled him,
the gesture his hand made
 when his mind made one
  great thought from two
  of a professor's ideas.
Cupping a handful of gelatin,
 gray and convoluted,
the lecturer shrugged and dropped it,
"Is this the seat of knowledge? — this organ? —
Is this the soul writ here in nerves and ganglia?
No one knows."

The orbs of Frankenstein replied
"I am the one who *will* know."

Hunched in the darkest nook
 of the students' wine cellars
I heard him complain,
 "It's not enough to watch
those well-rehearsed dissections.
If only I had a cadaver —
 one of my own —
I must know the inner workings of life!"

How could I bear to hear him suffer,
 he who should want nothing?
That night I robbed a mausoleum —
a rich man's grave easy to plunder,
a simple job of claw and crowbar,
 a lumpy sack and a handcart.
I dumped the sack before his door and knocked.
He came in nightshirt, candle in hand,

<267>

looked down at me in startlement.
"For you," I said. "Your own
c—-c——ca—-cadaver," I stammered.

He did not seem surprised. He took
one end of the heavy burden, let me
come in with the rest of it.
"It's very fresh," I assured him.
"He was only interred just yesterday."

I waited. He stared at me.
"How much do you want?" he asked.
"Oh, nothing!" I answered.
"You must want something for this!"
"I want...I want." I could not say it.
"Tell me." He looked a little kind, then.
I think he understood.
"I want to serve you," I told him.
    "Serve you...always."

3
We worked on happily —
    my shovel and cart,
    his saw and scalpel.
We found a more remote
    and spacious laboratory,
paid for with gold
    (how I laughed
    as I melted each crucifix,
    stripped village churches
    of their gilded adornments!)
I turned the wheels
    that made small lightning
    leap over the ceiling vault.

I bellowed the gas
    that lightning condensed
    into the glowing elixir

<268>

that made life scream
into inanimate matter.

Our workroom was madhouse —
old vellum books and amulets
heaped up with bones of animals,
crystal and astrolabe,
the surgeon's shining tools,
the charnel pit
    of amputated limbs.

In madness we succeeded.
    We howled
as tissues dead or rotting
quivered and multiplied,
as hands flew off
in every direction,
    eyes rolled
    and irises dilated
    in lidless horror,
brains roiled
in their captive tanks,
their spine stems twitching
with inexpressible longings.

Then we threw all
into a vat of acid.
"These are but preludes,"
he confided to me.
"What next?" I asked.
"Shall we raise the dead?"

"No, Fritz, I have no use
for the rotting dead. Most men
are little more than animated meat,
unfit for the one life given them.

"We shall make a being new,
a *manufactured man*."

<269>

So raptured was he,
    that saying this,
he fell down senseless.

I put him in bed,
    undressed his senseless form,
stroked the white limbs
    no scalpel had scarred,
then limped to my corner
where I slept like a dog,
like some great hound
who had found his god.

4
Then *she* came — Elizabeth.
At first I hated her.
Her finery mocked me, her manners
impeccable, her accent *just so*.
Though he had never mentioned her,
they were betrothed, in love
since childhood, it seems.

Daily she came for tea,
tried to win me over
with pastries and gingerbread,
plied Victor for news
of his abandoned studies.

As one upon another
each Ingolstadt don
came up for our mockery
(except our idol Waldman)
her awe increased.

I liked her laughter,
the way blond hair exploded
when she threw off her bonnet,
the Alpine sky in her eyes.

<270>

Yet I hated to watch
her chaste little kisses
that fell on Victor's blushing cheeks,
they way their hands
would find each other.
One day we were alone.
I had to make excuses
while Victor dissected
a youthful suicide
we'd fished from a stream,
his copy of *Werther*
still in his pocket.

Then she told me
    she was an orphan too,
    her name not Frankenstein
        like those who raised her
        as Victor's "cousin,"
    but Lavenza.
Frau Frankenstein had found her,
one of five babies in a hovel,
kept by peasants
    to whom she'd be
    a careworn Cinderella.
She was a fairy child,
raised by the Frankensteins
on music and poetry.

She knew nothing of what we did.
The sight of blood, the surgeon's saw
would fill her with horror.
How could she hope to companion
this man who walked with gods?

And then it happened.
She touched me.
A passing thing, really.
A piece of gingerbread
from palm to palm,

<271>

but then she lingered,
pressed fingers against
my inner palm.
"You are so loyal to Victor,"
she said,
"so you shall be dear to me."
She never flinched
at my twisted visage.
Her eyes saw past
the hump and its shadow.

Dear to her! Dear to her!
That night I scaled
the boarding house wall,
watched from a tree
as she undressed,
then drank some warm milk
at her bedside.
I watched in slice of moonlight,
her breasts and bosom
in lonely heaving,
her legs this way and that.
Had Victor ever lain with her?
Might I, "dear friend?"
Next night the milk
was tinged with laudanum.
I crept beneath
her silken beddings,
buried my face
in her virgin globes—
oh, I was light upon her,
like the fairies she dreamt of.
Once she cried out,
    "Oh, Victor!"

I stole away,
    the scent of her golden nape,
    those wondrous nipples
    with me always.

<272>

5

Next night more laudanum
was in Victor's red wine,
cheap vintage we bought
to celebrate the surgery
by which the suicide's heart
now beat in a headless torso.

I carried him to bed,
removed the blood-stained smock,
sponged off his fevered brow,
watched him in candlelight
as his features softened,
his eyelids fluttering
in pulse of dream-state.
I lay beside him,
touching, oh! everywhere.
Twice he cried out;
once, he held me
without awakening.

I crept away in bliss,
mad as a moth in a lamp shop.
Now, when they talk of marriage
it is a happy thought.
I can be wed to both of them
as long as the laudanum holds out.

6

Damn the chemist! The sleeping draught
wore off at the worst of times.
The master knows all. He woke from his sleep
as I perched at the foot of his bed.
My nakedness repelled him. He hurled
me out of his window into a haycart,
damned me, warned me never
to return to my room in the cellar.

<273>

What could I do? To whom could I go?
I took a whip from the half-wrecked cart,
climbed up the stairs to the empty laboratory.

He would need me when he ascended.
A storm was coming soon. The lifeless shell
up there was nearly ready for animation.
I would hand him the whip.
I'd beg him to punish me, hurt me,
but let me stay for the great work.
I wanted to see his eyes
    as his being stood before him,
hear his cry of god-defying blasphemy
    as man took control,
and named the day of the dead's arising.

7

My god and punisher returned.
He found the whip, and used it.
For days I lay not moving,
    my lacerating flesh alive,
    my blood congealing
to the scabs I was proud to wear,
the stripes of his forgiveness.

He sent me out on a sacred quest:
a pair of kidneys but hours dead,
a male, with "everything intact."
I understood what was needed.
As I prowled the street for drunkards
I conceived a monstrous jest.

Our being must be superlative,
and I knew just the man.
Jean-Christophe Weiss was the talk
of every student in the beer hall.
He boasted of his conquests,
how women fainted
    beneath his exertions.

<274>

The Ingolstadt brothel would not admit him
    unless he paid a triple rate.
Mothers warned daughters to turn away
when his languid gaze caught them.
Their faces reddened as he shopped the stalls,
one hand on an apple or a loaf of bread,
the other lifting a veil, or a skirt.
It was said that certain widows
happily opened their doors to him.
One night he leaped from the balcony
of the nunnery of St. Genevieve's
and what had happened there
not one of the sisters would tell.

I did not wait long to find him.
Like me, he knew how
    to evade the curfew.
I caught him emerging
from a certain garden gate
(a house with three comely daughters).
One blow to the head
with my crowbar,
then into the sack he went.)

The surgery was flawless.
Once more I watched
as disconnected tissues,
loose veins and nerves
like roots from a flowerpot
quivered, electrified,
sought one another
like amorous eels
and *connected*,
how the rent flesh closed
beneath the sutures:
weeks of healing
completed in minutes!

<275>

If Victor recognized
the organs' donor,
he never showed it.
I know he looked
again and again

as our perfect being's
perfect manhood
rose and fell
    rose and fell,
as vein and synapse
made their connections.

"Cover him!"
he said at last.
"My God,
    what a monster!"

8

"The kites, Fritz! The kites!"
With these words all
was forgiven — he needed me.
The howling storm raged.
Day became night as roiling thunder heads
collided like contending Titans,
black rams butt-heading the Alps
    and one another.
The rain came down
   in undulating sheets, blown
      this way, that way.
Right over us, two airborne lakes
smashed one upon another's cheek
and fell, exploding. Roulades
of thunder echoed everywhere.
Streams became torrents, meres rose
and swallowed astonished sheep and cattle.
As every shutter in Ingolstadt
clamped shut, we knew the day
was ours. No one would see

<276>

the sloping roof of our old mill tower
slide open to the elements,
or how the scaffolding rose up,
and I within it, high as the steeples.
From safe within my insulated cage
I unfurled the kites on their copper wires.
Up they went, hurled eastward,
then back again in gales contrary,
till they soared taut and defiant,
over the blackened granite hill
whose woods surrounded our workplace.

I did not fear the lightning.
I sang to it, danced it down.
"Strike! Strike!" I screamed.
"Come now, ye flames of Heaven!
Waste not your energy
    on those pitiful pines.
I am the bait,
    so come for me —
I am King of the Gargoyles —
I am deformity incarnate —
blasphemer since infancy —
robber of graves and churches —
rapist and fornicator!"
I was the spider, the wires
    my webs to lure God down.

It came! I howled
as the great light jabbed toward me,
reveled in the thunder's drum,
exulting as the kites survived
lash after lash, boom upon boom.
Blue, green and amber sparks
    spun, danced and plummeted.
I could not see below,
but I knew what was happening:
how Victor captured it all
in those vast and hungry capacitors,

<277>

how the hot wires sparked and smoked
as the current transferred
to the vat of green elixir
in which our creature bathed —
how all its flesh, unable to die
(and yet thus far without the will
to live) would join the ranks of creation.

How long I played there,
tempting with soliloquies
    the angry sky,
how long the kites
drew power downward
till they fell in tatters
I cannot tell.
I was deafened and nearly blind
when the master drew me down.
He led me to my corner,
said I would see in a while.
My ears already made out
the master's song of victory
as he cried out "It's *alive*!
    It's *alive*!"

He robbed the gods
of more than fire or gold —
my master, *Frankenstein,*
the modern Prometheus!

<278>

Nights at the Strand

The Strand Theater, Scottdale, PA

As the lights dim and the tattered curtain
rustled and parted with a creak-crank
of unseen wheels and pulleys, as a boy's eyes
widen to a dark screen grown suddenly bright
and huge — not the tiny ovoid TV
but vast, enormous, spanning the width
of his field of vision from Row Three,
the row, as Marilyn tells him
with a fifth-grader's knowing accent
where the monsters are in perfect focus.
He cleans his glasses furiously
as the sound track crackles, and a globe
topped with the RKO tower emanates
a zig-zag of Marconi waves, and, lo,
he commences his movie-watching Saturdays
with *King Kong,* who, on that screen,
amid those shrieks and screams of the crowd

<279>

on-screen and in the audience, strides tall
on his island, taller yet as he scales
the uncountable floors of the Empire State.
He had seen cartoon dinosaurs, but those
who try to wrest the Fay Wray-morsel from Kong
are as real as they get, the first taste
of a primal world of eat-and-be-eaten,
smite-or-be-smitten, the first beware
of the fate of him who falls for Beauty.

An old poet now, on a far coast, he can, if asked,
recite all the names of the movies he saw there
like a litany, week by week, in double-feature pairs,
as dear to him as the saint days to a medieval monk.
A basement full of surgical failures in *The Black Sleep* –
first view of an exposed brain a special thrill.
They do that to crazy people in Torrance, he's told,
skull-top raised up like an egg-cup, brains
poked and stirred around for no more reason
than *Let's see what happens if we do this*.
The mute sad butler played by Lugosi was a pathetic sight;
the man who had been Dracula reduced to a doorman.
Rathbone and Carradine, Tamirov and Johnson
the mad doctor and his henchmen and victims.
This double-billed with *The Creeping Unknown*,
whose alien-microbed astronaut, gaunt and wandering
assimilates all life in its path: men, cacti and lions,
until it oozes octopoid onto the scaffolding
around Westminster Abbey. Fast work
for stalwart scientist Quatermass who rigs
the metalwork with a million volts
from a nearby power plant.

After *The Blob* he turned inward to his chemistry set
and devised, with his friends, The Boron Monster,
     a bubbling mess
of boric acid, carbonates, and a medley of insect parts
that festered for two days in a Florence flask, then
made a nocturnal exeunt into the floor drain. For weeks

<280>

the four boys of the Kingview Science Club swore they heard it
in house pipes and gurgling drains; one went so far
as to say it raised its white pseudopods when he looked
into the late-night toilet bowl.
                          The dreaded Cyclops
from *The Seventh Voyage of Sinbad* seemed as he woke
to stand in silhouette against the bare hill behind his house.
When the garish colors of *Curse of Frankenstein*
reveled in blood and bosoms, he set up shop
in Caruso's garage in Keiffertown. *Live Monster Show,*
the hand-drawn poster said in drip-red lettering
and the children came from all around.
Clothesline and sheet for curtain, old 78
of *The Sheik of Araby* a Gothic foxtrot,
his fellow fourth-graders no longer chemists
but grease-paint actors: monster and villagers,
doctor and hunchback. Naturally *he* is the Doctor,
his hands the ones that raise Jell-O brains and send blood
rivulets down the aisles among the screaming girls.
A raincoat, sleeves inverted, can pass for a Dracula cape.
He sends for a mail order course in hypnotism.
They learn the art of mummy-wrapping (green chalk
and Noxema), black powder and kerosene for fires,
dry ice for malevolent Jekyll-Hyde elixirs.

But there's no keeping up with the Strand and its
accelerating horrors. The bugs have invaded:
ant and tarantula, mantis and locust grown
to the size of locomotives, the dark side
of the atom whose giant flower mutations
they are taught about on schooldays. They would
all glow in the dark and in perfect health
when Our Friend the Atom was done with them.
After *Them!* and *Tarantula, Beginning of the End,*
The Giant Claw, and *The Deadly Mantis,*
the worst was *The Black Scorpion,* so horrible,
in fact, that as he watched it open a train
like a sardine can, extract the passengers, then sting
them with its terrible stinger before the slow

<281>

ascent to the drooling jaws and mandibles, someone
on the balcony vomited a visual melange
of popcorn and orange soda on his brother's shoulders.

Then came Godzilla, a whole new order
of urban destruction and radium-breath:
boys who had never seen a city looked on
as powerlines and factories, gas terminals and seaports,
glass and steel towers, department stores and palaces
were stamped to splinters and rubble
beneath the wayward reptilian scourge
that had nothing to do with eating: Godzilla was hell-rage,
a force that might wipe clean the earth once and forever
of the human infestation.
                              Godzilla was manifest, too,
in the form of a fat bully on Mulberry Street
who waited to knock the school and library books
from his hands into the nearest snowdrift.
He filled a squirt gun with ammonia and onion juice,
a minor armament since he was studying nuclear fission
and knew a dozen withering curses in Latin.
The bully fades from memory — he must,
at least once, have used the gun against him.

When the saucers of *The Mysterians* began airlifting women
to help repopulate a dying world, he was jealous,
dreamt of a gravity beam abduction from his own bed.
Forbidden Planet taught him to embrace the alien:
if left on Altair Four he'd happily join Morbius
in solitary study of the long extinct Krell geniuses;
if taxed enough with unjust bullying, he'd join
the crew of Nemo's Nautilus: they'd all be sorry
when he sank half the Atlantic fleet or turned
the submarine to starship and beat the Russians to Mars.
He had never been two towns away,
    but he knew the names of the outer planets' moons.

<282>

Small boy in torn shoes and baggy hand-me-downs
sewn from his father's old shirts,
goggle-eyed with wrong glasses, arms full
of comics and all the books he could carry,
he was The Strand's acolyte, its screen and stage
the doorway to a higher reality. No matter
how far he has gone, what written or done,
he is still there, in that seat in Row Three
as the ships land, the invasion commences,
the tentacle comes slowly into focus
at the edge of vision, the branches part
to those two great orbs of The Beast.

He was the one who ran away
    to join the Monsters
        to explore the stars,
haunted, to become the Haunter.

<283>

Something There Is In the Attic

Every human body is a haunted house.
Something there is in the attic
that drives it and sets it course.
Are the shutters half-drawn?
Are they nailed against sunrise?
Do spiders spin in the tenantless rooms?
Who lives there? Ahab and his mono-
Moby madness? Emily with her dry-
leaf poems like money under a bed?
Or no one at all? Does no one hear
as each flaked shingle falls,
as varicose ivy beards up, as sun
and sag gray-wash the porch beams
and lintels? Something there is
in the attic that drives it and
sets its course. Whose will? An old
man's will? A boy's? A loud-mouthed
betrayer of dreams? A dreamer
paralyzed? Why does this house
not fall, but stand at elmward avenue,
accusing all, begging a moon,
a clean sweep, a neighbor's knock,
a letter? Something there is
in the attic that drives it and
sets its course. This house is
Ahab's ship, Usher's manse, Lovecraft's
infirmary, a witch house, feast
hall, love nest and chapel, sanctum
of Solitude, the Capulets' tomb.
If every human body is a haunted
house, shall we not choose
these ghosts? Can I not summon
a typing poltergeist, a coloratura
howler, a phantom raconteur
to teach me all dead languages,
a gourmet chef insomniac,

<284>

someone for whom the 1812 Overture
has not (as for me) ever lost its charm,
a friend who hovers over Batman comics
and knows every line poor Bela Lugosi
was ever made to utter? Room enough,
and beds, and food and tea, for them all!

In October this house is avalanched,
as leaves, and ghosts of leaves
from every tree that ever crisped
in the tug between slant-sun and frost,
pile high in ziggurats of oak,
maple and sumac, hawthorn and willow,
each with a tale of hope and sorrow
waiting its turn for harvest.
They almost obscure the house, so high
that one lone cupola, the poet's watch,
stands apex at its pyramid,
as one mad vane whirls at the whim
of indecisive winds, as lightning rod
trembles for discharge of the weighted sky
into the attic haunter's cranium.

I am that attic Something: I drive
this house unchanging, wall-to-wall
with mad cargo. My gambrel roof
is an upside-down Mayflower
as I sail against the leaf-tide. Monsters
would block my passage: great whales
of Doubt breach above a maple current;

the baleful skyward eye and tentacles
of the giant squid of Loneliness float by
in a sea-tide of weeping willow.

<285>

Yet something there is in the attic
that billows the sails, and drives me on.
The madness that fills these pages
is self-sustaining: some days
these scratchings seem meaningless,
unmusical; some days I read and gasp
and shudder to think that somehow I wrote
or was written through, to reach this apogee.
Alone? Well, lacking the guests
I crave, I must split and become them.
Books, cat and bed, a galaxy of music,
teapot that fills as fast as I empty it:
it is not a bad life,
to be the haunter of one's cobwebbed self.

<286>

Since the Old Ones Came Back to Earth

for H.P. Lovecraft's Birthday, August 20, 2009

Since the Old Ones came back to Earth,
many awaken bruised with a dim sense
of having sleepwalked, some even
appalled to find themselves
eye to eye in a canopied bed
with an equally astonished stranger;
some find themselves in half
their bedclothes, their blood-caked
fingers twined 'round the shreds
of someone's exotic lingerie, a child's
underwear, or a tuft of animal hair.
The morning mirror exam sends some
in a quick cab to the emergency room
at the sudden onslaught of hives
bearing an uncanny resemblance
to the sucker marks of an octopus,
or a face full of spiderbites,
or the distinct feel beneath the skin
as burrowing leaf-litter bugs
take up residence, eat and lay eggs;
or the incessant sneezing of one
who has passed the night in a graveyard,
acquiring minute nasal centipedes.
Doctors have diagnosed a "cosmic malaise";
Blue Cross and United have declared it
an existential pre-existing condition,
exempting only Congress and the military.

Since the Old Ones came back to Earth,
last year's brown leaves are not replaced
with new ones, and breadloaf *fuligo*,
world's largest slime-mold, ripens
putrescently 'round tree roots.

<287>

No one has ever seen
 so many mushrooms
in so many shapes and hues.
Wheat sprouts to rust, the rye to must,
young fruit to the fringe of mildew;
the produce counter is a filamented web
of blue mold, white mold, black *aspergilis*.
Old folks idling on benches, or babies
left unattended by gossiping nannies
are found enwebbed by barn spiders
the size of house cats. At sea it's worse,
as fishing boats hang in weed-clog,
cruise liners picked clean of edible beings
by hunting pods of ammoniac squid.
The warming globe proves Darwin right,
as new and ambulating gilled Things
begin to move among us,
and want brides; as yogurt mutates
into an aggressive arborial blob
whose pseudopods seek out
and throttle the city's songbirds.

Hundreds swear they have been carried aloft
by faceless things that hugged and humped them
as strong talons held them immobilized;
crazed Carmelite nuns go belly-huge,
they claim, from angelic fetal implants.
Here in the city's wolf-hour orgies,
sleepwalkers mingle with wide-awake molesters,
who in their turn are seized
 by invisible tentacles.
Everyone has been a sex toy for something,
from every conceivable angle.

<288>

Awake, each looks at all with alarm
and embarrassment. When pregnancies
arise — and they are frequent now —
no woman knows who the father is,
or even if it's human. Just being gay
seems trivial against the thought
of twenty-organ sex, spread out
across all neurons, pulsing the span
from infrared to gamma rays.

Life, since the Old Ones came back to Earth,
means every sense and orifice
is violated: passive and paranoid
we dread the nightfall, the drowsy pillow.
Our telescopes have penetrated the universe;
now we in turn are raped by space.

<289>

Midnight Water

THINGS TOLD
        to frighten children:
        Never drink water
        at the stroke of midnight —
        you'll choke,
fall dead of a heart attack —
this happened to one
of your many cousins.

We lay awake
at grandmother's house,
no one going to the kitchen,
no one lifting
the dented tin cup,
the old enamel dipper.

Even if midnight waters
didn't kill —
            in the dark
a bug might be there,
a hairy caterpillar,
a centipede sipping,
ready to be swallowed,
or a chunk of moss
from the cold spring,
floating unseen in the bucket,
sliding like slug
into the dipper.

<290>

Pitch black nights
the grandpa clock
ticked and chimed
above the wheezes and snores.
The whippoorwills called,
waiting like you
for the pre-dawn hours,
the safe water.

<291>

Milkweed Seeds

The air is full of milkweed seeds —
they fly, they light, they fly again —
they cling to leaf, and cat-tail,
dog fur and hedgehog quill.

They burst out of pods like wizened hags,
white hair pluming on witch winds.
Do not be fooled by their innocent pallor:
the sour milk sac that ejected them
is made of gossip, spite and discord.
Pluck this weed once, two take its place,
roots deep in the core of malice.

Cousins to carrion flower and pitcher plants
they fall on sleepers who toss in misery,
engendering boils and bleeding sores.
These are no playful sprites of summer —
they go to make more of their kind —
and if one rides through an open window
it can get with child an unsuspecting virgin,
who, dying, gives birth to a murderer.
Just give them a wind
      that's upward and outward
and they're off to the mountains
to worship the goat-head eminence,
pale lord of the unscalable crag,

Evil as white as blasted bone,
his corn-silk hair in dreadlocks,
his fangs a black obsidian,
      sharp as scalpels,
his mockery complete
as every dust mote sings his praises.

Do not trust white, winged and ascending to heaven!
Beware, amid the bursting flowers, the sinister pod!

<292>

Whom None But the Shattered Stones Recall

THEIR CONCRETE MARVELS
shall not stand!
These engineers who drain and brick
the land so leveled by ice, so slaked
with the forgetting of mountains—
the glacial waters are wary of them—
their digging will not avail.
The frog shall return, and men relinquish
their crumbling walls to floods subterrane.
Dark streams shall turn, and limestone seas
burst from their ancient vaults, triumphant.

Then sleeping Mystery, ice-fanged,
entangled in the roots of trees, worm-fed
from the bottoms of sepulchres,
shall stretch itself awake in fog,
gracing their doorsteps with its name.
Its hair shall cling to steeple tops,
its voice shall peal in the Sunday bells,
crackle beneath the boom of radios,
jack hammer drumming its warbeat call.

Earth, you were wild once: you shall be
    wild again.
Lap at this masonry, wrinkle the parking lot
    with giant's shrug,
consume their trucks in a midnight seizure
    of maelstrom mud.
Return the swamp to the gods who made it,
    to the tortoise,
    to the dream-dealing bats
    to the panther fire of whirling gas
    moondancing on lily pads

<293>

To the Spirit of this place: The Entangled One,
breaker of tomahawks and kindler of council fires,
ensnared by Christian tombs and the steel
     tanks of gasoline —

To the Spirit of this place: The Entangled One,
dreamer of forbidden dreams, alive beyond
     the tangent
where a line meets the curve of the infinite circle;
nascent as the fork of trees aches for a lightning touch;
fatal to know yet impossible to avoid —
To the Spirit of this place: The Entangled One,
swim up from your ice-bound caverns locked
since the thundering glacier's age,
by the name that the ash-fire Indian knew you —
     mighty Atotarho, death-wielding
     chief and sorcerer —
whom none but the shattered stones recall—
return!

Ghosts

Ask ghosts if there's a Heaven
or if they linger here to haunt
because the lips of Hell
fire-tongue the fringe
of their continuance.

Why need to loiter
in chill old mansions,
in potter's fields,
dank woods and fens,
in crenellated ruins,
if Paradise tugs
at the gowns of the dead?

Ask any ghost if he
would rather be alive!

<294>

Whippoorwill Road

WHY HAVE THESE WOODS,
          which yesterday
acknowledged me, now shut me out?
The boughs that nodded to our songs
hang limp today in molten dusk;
          old trees that stood as monuments
loom sinister upon that hill
where but a day ago we sang.
I touch a tree — cold bark and moss
touch back, as if to write on me
their melancholic air of doom.

What drove me, on the brink of storm,
     to walk these paths?
I see no sign of animals. Even at dusk
this wood was full of treetop calls and scamperings,
bats dipping down to skim the creek, the fight for worms
among the forest birds, the cheery bacchanal
of matrimonial squirrels. But all of that
was yesterday. Today a barricade of burrs
deters my forward steps — I seek another route
back to the house, the comfort of a waiting fire.
By the sun, it seems I walk in circles, it seems
the thorns are mocking me toward some secret grove
some passageway a nymph or demon has laid me.

The infinite blue above me goes gray
as homing thunder heads assume the sky.
Gods! let these ancient, jagged trees not make
me target for their falling blades of fire!
Let them resolve among themselves which ones
shall burn tonight, which ones shall bear the stripe,
the sap's blood lashing of the nearing storm!
I do not wish to be the arbiter —
or worse, the bait — of dueling thunderbolts.

<295>

I find the fence between thicket and farm.
So close! the stone hut's windows beaming
sliced yellow bands across the bristling field.
Behind my back the pelting rain begins
and howling wind invades the deepest hollows.

A cloud-clot of brown-specked wings arises,
a V-shaped, angry pyramid of birds,
heedless of deadly air — or charged by it —
whistling the penetrating calls reserved
for witch-elm tangle and desolate shrubs,
disconsolate cry of the whippoorwills.
They circle the tumble-down chimney top,
bloated, dusty, disheveled as Harpies,
red-eyed owls crushed flat as on an anvil,
road-kill crushed by a heartless creator,
birds no other mother could hatch and keep.
Cursed Whippoorwills! tree-shunned Quasimodos,
Eastern hermits of heath and underbrush,
what brings you to the very roof I seek
as shelter from this arching, angry storm?

They ring the house, swoop in ever smaller
arcs of ominous descent. I start to run . . .

And then, remembering the tale, slow down
as chokefire breath burns in my throat and feet
conspire to hook on every rabbit hole.
No use to run. Useless the word or charm,
in vain the loaded gun against them now.
Another something shall rise in the storm,
something these birds shall catch and feed upon.
I know I'll find my old friend seated there
eyes over his book, hand poised at page-turn,
silent and still, just moments dead, soulless,
the better part of him gone up the flue,
torn in a clutch of beaks and talons.

<296>

All night, in wake of diminishing storm,
I hear them sing triumphantly: *Whip! Whip!*
Whip! Poor! Will! Whip! Poor! Will! Poor Will! Poor Will!
Whip Poor Will! Somewhere in those distant woods
in a witch-elm not touched by lightning thrust,
they have him now, their dry-leaf withered nests,
their luminous eggs draped with his memories,
hung with the scraps of his intelligence.
Night breeds, and hoards, and feeds its young
the harvest of souls, storm-snatched from the living.
Whip! Whip! Whip! Whip Poor Will! Whip!
   Whip Poor Will!

<297>

The Skeptic

October again. Out in the country you
    go to sleep. The leaves lap noisily at
    window ledge, rasping their tongues'
    red dust and ash onto the bedroom sill.
Down from the pines, the driving wind
roars in the spaces where you had been
before the frost endowed you with
indoor preferences. Wearied,
the bats prepare to hibernate, tuck chins
in breasts, fold heads into the overlaps
of wings, and sleep. Orion ascends
and strides the latticework of trees.
Somewhere, the water is turbulent,
somewhere, the beat of wings,
the blot of dark immensities
against an ochre moon;
somewhere the Dream who walks
the treetops and enshrines you
with its nightmare forms
weaves tentacles from stump
to trunk, to upper branch, dragging
itself to bask its single eye in wind.
You dream to give it life,
your little slice of death
its nascent bloom.

It squats in the dark of your
disbelief. It has your name.

<298>

By Moonlight, Surely, They'll Dance

Lean back against this gravestone.
   John will not mind, so long
   as ye utter your quiet thoughts.
   Tell him, as I have, of stars;
   how tonight the huge Dipper
bows to the lake; of houses
where none stood a hundred
years ago, those firm lights

<299>

gleaming on the west shore.
He'll weep not if you tell him
a man can still paddle north,
lose sight of the lake behind
and consider the infinite.
Tell him, too, that Jeanette,
whom his loveless hand forgets,
lies still beside him and waits.

Come here with whatever beauty
the world offers, with his or her
kiss roll sweetly in this grass,
inflamed by her surrender, held
fast in his arms as he enfolds you,
go naked, starry proud, erect,
spill love's libations on this earth,
remind these hungered dead of their
    spring, let the seed
of your youth go wormlike to their
    joyless lips and wombs

Come alone, when September cools
and warns this ground of sleep.
Mark for these old, old lovers
how the wall has collapsed,
how conjunct earth and waves
have worn away the hillside;

tell them, not long now
till they love, falling free
of their tombs to the lulling shore,
how their lipless skulls shall kiss
and by moonlight, surely, they'll dance.

How they'll hide in the new grass
and watch the surly majesty of youth
repeating their ancient caresses —
not long, o pioneers

<300>

May Eve

I stalked the yews of that old hill
   which townsmen shun but for the final sleep,
   alone, I thought, until I saw the gleam
   of wind-whipped torches at the ridge.
   I stopped amongst the green-black pines
   which lean imperiled by the bog,
to watch the silent phantoms, all in white,
their street shoes and their trousers showing
as the wind, betraying, made them men.
They bore a box of unstained pine
upon a tattered velvet pall.
The wind — it should have borne their sighs
or words, but carried none — the crack
of torch wood and the brush of cloth
were all I heard. Before a vault,
a mausoleum with its name effaced,
they lay their burden on the ground.
To hear what rites they might pronounce,
what curious dead they so interred,
I crept across the stone-toothed lawn
to but a yard from they pried
the locks from off the rusted door.
A groan of hinge. I saw the black
unwindowed room which swallowed them,
a room whose floor was an open gate
into the limestone hill, where torches,
twelve in all, receded, until the black,
black silence deceived me. Had I dreamt this?
Would I wake at dawn in cemetery grass
alone as ever in this neglected spot?

But here, the open door. I stepped
up to the verge. I dared not cross
this threshold into ultimate knowing.
I heard them, then. They were not
mute as they had been. They sang —

<301>

not words I knew — it was a chant,
rising and falling to a hideous drone —
I heard a hammer blow,
a rending of nails out of wood,
and then, what echoed from the cave below:
that nameless *Feast* until the dawn!

Todesblumen

A woman is dying inside,
nestled in quilts and soft pillows.
On the path from the spring,
lit by the eye of an elder moon,
her nephew returns with full wooden buckets.
By the barn, he stares at the tarpapered house.
The kerosene light from the sick room
falls on a trellis: he sees what the women
had whispered about in the kitchen —
that rose abloom in December.
(They reverted to German, called it
Todesblumen, death's flower bloom,
would not speak of it where Aunt Lena lay,
though she might see, if she looked, a yard
from the house, where it opened.)
Raising his buckets to clear a snowdrift,
the boy hastens by the sickbed window, and there —
white, whiter than snow, without shadow,
but solid, a stark figure steps into the light.
From shapeless robes a skeletal hand emerges:
the shivered rose crumbles, falls petal by petal.
The hand extends further on ghost-white fore-arm.
Now at the window comes the tap-tap-tapping
of Death, and wind, and the barren trellis
shakes. Then nothing, and silence, and then
the keening cry from the women inside.

<302>

An Expectation of Presences

"To die is far different from what anyone supposed...
and luckier."— Walt Whitman

HIS GRAVESITE, phantomless, does not appease
my walk — not for myself alone
have I come, but in an expectation
of presences drawn forth like tides
from that alluring moon, to sit
and hear the chattering of ghosts
for the dead must have many songs to sing:
their dire complaints, their unrequited loves,
their broken oaths, their bony fists
clenched in the earth for some unsweet revenge;
their pleas that some neglected deed be done
to free them from a wormy pilgrimage;
their wry requests to know what souls
once famed to them, now call such pits
a hearth. But here's no tombly talk;
none but a nightbird and a tapping branch
reply to my arcane soliloquy.

My eyes, as keen
for darkness as those of an owl,
spy nothing; my ears, keen
almost to the ultrasonic
hear nothing but the bird-stir
and the limestone lap of lakebed.

Where are the ghosts?
These peaceful dead, this tranquil town
sleep far too well reposed.
        Doubts do not stalk
these penny plots, no killers wring
remorseful hands, not one protesting atheist
is doomed to somnambulist stumbling.

<303>

Can it be
that in their simple times
(the whole of the 1800s buried here!)
mere faith could be a perfect opiate,
that life within a wall of hymns
led to this silent, dreamless death?

Ah, so they die, who *believe* in Death,
they never rise, who sell their souls
into a cleric's dull paradise;
they never fly, who think their wings
are promises, to be attached
in worlds not one can wake to see.
O fraud of frauds, and no recourse:
no lawyer can sue an evangelist.

Yet in my heart of hearts I wish
for ghosts. For here is the depth
of all possible woe —
to leave *nothing* behind,
nothing to strain against stars
from the haunted tips of trees;
nothing to drift like summer heat
and catch a gable's underside;
nothing to gust from cellar doors
or brood with the trunks in the attic;
nothing to serve as a core for leaves
as they fly in autumn deviltry;
no remnant left to walk the town,
no shadow over the bed, no chill
or mystery for the nervous ones —
those living yet
    who think they see the dead —
to be lost from the hands of conjurers,
not even a gleam, a shard
of phosphorescent ooze?

<304>

Oh, no, if the choice be
God's heaven or earth-bound ghost,
I'll keep my anchorage to moonlit nights,
take deed to swamps and vacant lots,
turn houses to renounced estates
abandoned to fright's hostelry;
sunbathe on monuments,
dance wild in summer thunderstorms.

Then, I shall wait for the night
when a dreaming poet comes
to my scarcely-legible tombstone,
mad as myself, my laughing heir.
What things I shall whisper
into his modern, doubting, skeptical
ear, as I reach out ...
        and take his hand.

<305>

Sinkholes

i

They called it *The Swamp,*
and although much of the lakeshore
was wetland, weed- and frog-
infested, lily-pad-mosquito-land,
everyone knew, when you said it
with that certain intonation
voicing italics *and* initial caps,
that you meant *The Swamp.*
It was a pond, reed-fringed
water a shallow cover for floor
of mud from which noxious vapors
bubbled, and where foxfires glowed
on certain moonless nights.
Beneath the mud, though none could see it
was a water-filled cavern
of unknown depths. I was shown
the Geological Survey map whose legend
denominated a place with no known bottom.

Locals take that on faith:
for generations it's been the place
where useless vehicles, scrap iron
and dead refrigerators are dragged,
pushed with some danger to the townsmen
as they go knee-deep in sucking mud
until their offering is far enough in
for whatever it is that wants things
to begin its inexorable pulling.
Within a day an old jalopy
is nothing but two round headlights,
glass frog-eyes, then nothing
as by the next morning the swamp pool
resumes its perfect flatness, its mud
as uniformly flat as a well-made bed.

<306>

ii

I remember a field
we were not allowed to play in —
and playing there anyway
my friends and I discovered
the vertical maw into blackness
we learned was an abandoned mine.
One day it had been a cornfield;
the next the shaft had fallen in.
In a town criss-crossed with forgotten
mines, it could happen anywhere:
holes the size of pancakes, holes
just big enough to swallow a bully,
an arrogant preacher, a rival
(if only one could make them appear!)
Soft ground was best, but even
a sidewalk crack, a storm drain opening,
a gynasium floor or a toilet
could give way into a sinkhole,
a cenote, a sudden burst
of Karst topography. Someone you really
didn't like could be swept away
into an underground river or fall,
fall, fall beyond the length of rope
to a dull thud at the hard place
between the earth's crust and mantle.

We came back again and again to see it,
to test how black
its blackness could measure.
Tar, coal, obsidian, ink: nothing we knew
was blacker than this cavern-hole.
We threw soft coal, and chunks
of sharp obsidian, iron slag
and a 16-ounce soda bottle
as hard as we could from a safe overhang.
No echo answered our probing.
So far as we knew, it had no bottom,
as though the mine below

<307>

had been mined *from* below
by subterranean demons.
Although we stopped playing there
and walked a long way 'round
the hillock that humped over it,
in dreams we walked its maw-edge,
lost our bearing, missed one another's
outreached hand of rescue,
or were *pushed* —
and worse by far than the nightmare
of falling into it was the dread
of what might come out of it,
if it wanted to, and was hungry enough.
What if, at night, some shambling Thing
crept into our cellars, filling great sacks
from our coal bins, returning the fuel
to the mountain depths? What if we went,
as we sometimes did, to stoke the furnace
at the stroke of midnight
and came eye to eye with *It*?

iii
I read of places
where sink holes appear
without warning, some watered
beneath with underground rivers,
but others just chasms, cave vents
or rifts between two angry seams
of geologic tension. Cybele's
temple was just such a place,
its altar an opening into darkness .
that drove women mad, and men
to self-mutilation.
Just such a place
is the entrance to Tartarus,
nine days below Hell.

<308>

One falls, not into open space
like Milton's bad angels
(who enjoyed a feast of starlight
while they plummeted) —
but no, one falls
    into an ever-narrowing funnel
    of cold darkness,
into a place where legs
    and arms are useless
until there is nothing of you
    but a head screaming upwards
towards an ever-dwindling
    pinpoint of light.

Our earth is a shifting island of sea and magma,
Swiss-cheesed with sink holes, cenotes,
Blue Holes at the bottoms of coral seabeds —
Something riddled with Nothing,
orbiting a self-regulated explosion,
sun hurtling around and away from
the Black Hole at the rift of space-time,
Every moment of existence here averts
an infinity of empty, unpeopled stars.

<309>

DOCTOR JONES &
OTHER TERRORS

Doctor Jones

1

He drives a black Ford V8 Cabriolet.
It has a gold top, gold wheel spokes,
huge, round, cracked headlamps
glowing like yellow, bloodshot eyes.
His name is Alphonse Perry Jones.
That's *Doctor* Jones to you, little fellow.
He went to the War in Nineteen-Eighteen,
right out of medical school,
sent to the front in France
    with a black bag and a kit.
The soldier boys were brought in by the dozens.
The routine was simple — a swig of whisky
    the only anesthetic —
roll up the sleeves or the trouser cuffs.
Two men to pin the soldier down —
    he didn't mind the sawing.
He never vomited the way the aides did.
He didn't mind the screams. In fact
    he somewhat grew to enjoy them,
    phonemes of agony, no two alike.
His eyes that hadn't focused well
    on parting flesh and severed arteries
    now studied each push and pull,
almost a rhythm to the saw thrusts
    and the soldier's scream,
in and out almost

<310>

like lovemaking.
Sometimes the tourniquet and
    cauterizing took.
Sometimes they bled to death
    blubbering, eyes rolled
    to egg whites.
The nurses turned away. He
put his hand against the carotid
to feel the last spasms.

It looked like a benediction
but it was a taking —
    there, there it is,
    you're dead now.

After months at the Front,
dodging the Germans
and the gassy, shifting lines,
he is the only doctor left.
No one will eat with him.
The men whisper and stare,
sleep turned away
    with their guns loaded.
He does not care.
    They obey his orders.
The great tide of wounded keeps coming,
never enough crutches or bandages.
A hecatomb of hands and feet,
arms to the elbow, legs to the knee
fester unburied in a nearby trench.
Too bad the Armistice came so soon.

But that was long ago, years past
    and a drawer of tarnished medals
to prove he had been there, done that.

<311>

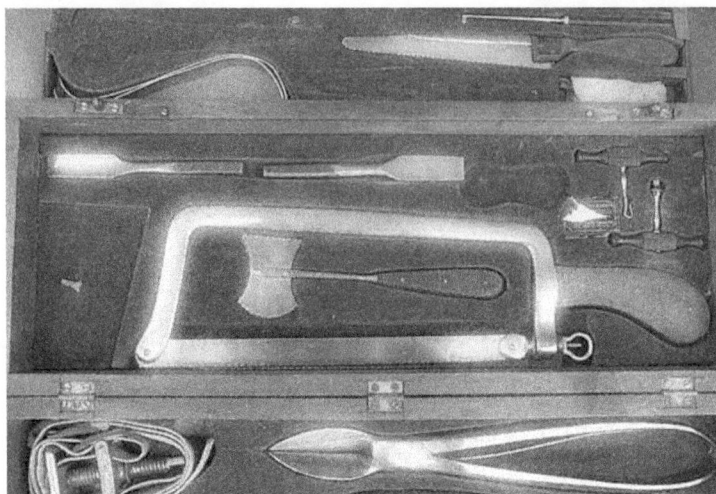

Late afternoon he rides
    the hills and hollows,
follows the yellow buses,
    watches the scrawny boys
    with their cowboy lunch boxes
    as they run to their mothers.

There beside him, his little book
with the names and addresses,
there,
        the black bag
            with everything he needs.
His name is Alphonse Perry Jones.
That's *Doctor* Jones to you, little fellow.
And he does house calls.

<312>

2

Five years ago I remembered you,
Doctor Jones. Five years ago
I tried to write this poem —
three times the pen
    touched down upon the empty page
three times
    my hands shook uncontrollably.

Are some things better not
remembered,
as flesh forgets wounds?
No, even flesh does not
forget: pale scars
are always there,
the ghosts of fractures
act up on rainy days.

We do not forget:
we crystallize around
our childhood terrors.

I see you, country doctor:
gaunt and cadaverous,
goateed and spectacled,
an old man towering
above my weakness.
Your fingers circle
my pencil-thin arms
as you chide my parents

Don't you feed this child?
He's all skin and bones.
Your cold hammer knocks
and my knees kick out at you,
the stethoscope,
so cold I stop breathing.
You send me home
with cod liver pills,

<313>

which now supplement
the government surplus meat
and cheese we live on.
Soon Mother shows me
your sinister car.

That's Doctor Jones, she says.
If you don't do what you're told
he'll come some night
and have your leg off.

3
I go to school now
in a place called Hecla.
The school door faces
the grim machineries
of a coal mine.

From the back
of the school bus
I sometimes see
your black Ford
behind our dust cloud.

Sometimes a boy gets off,
runs down a lane,
down which your car
makes a slow turn,
following.
I never see
how it ends.

<314>

When I come home,
the endless rumble
of coal trucks
feeding the coke evens
drowns out
the comings and goings
of your car,
but I know you are there.

More than one night
I spied those yellow headlights
with their tired veins glimmering,
slowing and stopping,
slowing and stopping
as though you watch
our windows for the darkout.

I will not sleep
where a door is open,
see gaunt and bearded specters
in the musty closets.
The rats in the cellar,
the giant spiders
in the blackness of the attic,
the quicksand pools
out back behind
the slagheaps,
are minor terrors
beside you.

That year I watched locusts
sprout by the thousands
from tree and earth,
endured a hurricane
that ripped the arms
from the Lombardy poplars,
saw my first movie
where Nemo's ship,
held fast by tentacles,

<315>

broke free of the giant squid
in a harpoon battle.

These things were as nothing
when my mother walked
to the telephone and said,
"All right, you little brat,
I'm calling Doctor Jones
right now!"

I hear myself still,
shrilly screaming,
bounding up steps,
closing my door,
waiting for the sound
of the gliding car.

Dark nights I sleepwalked
to escape you.

4
Five years ago I remembered you,
Doctor Jones. Five years ago
I tried to write this poem —
three times the pen
    touched down upon the empty page
three times
    my hands shook uncontrollably.

You are still everywhere:
    the doctor
    the dentist
    the barber, even, pressing me down
        in his innocent chair
you are still there
    in every unwanted touching.
You make every touch unwanted.

<316>

My mother is dead
and cannot erase you.
My father tells me you never existed,
that there was no doctor named Jones,
that no such name was ever spoken
    in his presence,
something your mother did to you,
some kind of mental abuse...

yet why do I know all three of your names,
the yellow-white bristles of your beard,
your medals and how you got them?
Why do I spy, within your plain black bag,
the reddish-brown leather
    of the American-made kit
    with its amputation bone saw,
    the finger saw,
    the metacarpal saw?

His name is Alphonse Perry Jones.
That's *Doctor* Jones to you, little fellow.
We'll have that leg off in no time.

<317>

Torrance

1

It had a name, and an associated dread.
Even small children knew of it:
   a place to be sent
   if you turned out crazy
     were deemed retarded
       touched yourself too often
   hurt someone   or killed your father
A place they emptied the jails into
   with that special class of men
   too evil to live with ordinary killers
A place where the deformed,
   the epileptic,
   the melancholic
were secreted away.

No one seemed ever
   to come back from Torrance.
Aunt Thelma went,
   a "nervous breakdown."
Her husband hastily
   remarried
   her cousin Irma
   (they could have been sisters).
If you went once
   to the sunny wardroom
   to check in on a relative
you probably never went again —
something about the screams
   from the floor below,
the vacant stare of the patients
sunning themselves,
scalp scars and skull concavities,
mumbling   drooling
or the loquacious residents
eager to share the fact

<318>

that they were Jesus, Jahweh
or Marie Antoinette,
or one's poignant plea
"What news from the Holy Land?
Have the Crusaders
    taken Jerusalem?"

White coat doctors
smoked in the corridors.
Strict nurses and burly attendants
kept everyone behaved.
You never quite understood
why suddenly they'd seize
a seemingly calm one

Now, now, you've done it again –
    Didn't I tell you? –
        It's off to your room now –
attendant waiting
    with that special jacket
        just at the edge of vision.

You never saw a syringe
but you knew,
if it were your lot
to come here,
endless needles would jab at you,
and you would wake screaming
in a padded place with but
    one window
and no one would hear you,
hear you
ever...

<319>

No, if you saw that once,
   you'd never be back to see
   Aunt Thelma,
your mouth dry
with the thought
They could keep me here,
   if only they knew —
      knew what I've done...

Built in 1919,
a red brick mansion
by any standard.
Handsome arches,
a dayroom lit
like a conservatory.
The director dined
on the finest linen and china,
the best food.
The doctors employed
the latest techniques.
Once you had signed away
the prisoner, the child,
   the broken-down wife,
they were free to experiment.

<320>

They opened skulls
    as smoothly
    as the director's wife
    scooped into a boiled egg,
poked around, sometimes removed
    a tumor or swelling.
If a criminal became
    a drooling idiot,
    what loss to society
if but one clue
to the brain's mysteries
were uncovered?

Then came the drugs,
and the Great Machine
that shock-erased bad memories,
    at least some of the time
        for some of the patients.
Too bad if they could no longer
remember their Shakespeare
or the best five years of their lives —
at least they were spared the knife.

Among the good doctors,
    a few were evil,
one, perhaps, as evil
as the jacketed murderers,

one, perhaps, who had been there
when the place opened
hard on the end
of the First World War.
He would have been a surgeon,
not qualified to touch
the seat of divinity the brain,
but there in reserve
when they hurt themselves
or one another, setting the bones,
stitching the flesh of would-be

<321>

suicides.
Once in a great while
an amputation was needed,
and he was ready
with his red-lined surgeon's case

    amputation saw
    metacarpal saws trephines
        and knives.

Just like the War! he would
say wistfully,
downing a whiskey
and shining his instruments.
This bone saw, he'd tell
his colleagues,
dates back to 1878,
fine British workmanship.

He didn't much like
the modern anesthetics,
was heard to say
There is a music to pain.

Perhaps for some years
he was the Night Doctor,
the only one who saw,
while the good staff
slept in their homes,
what a madhouse really is
when the moon hits it:

how the attendants,
for certain favors,
undid the doors,
and certain patients,
(even the murderers)
got into rooms
and did what they wanted —

<322>

or what was wanted —
in the rooms of others,
how there were dances
and music,

and the attendants
laughed as they set
the mad against the feeble-minded,
the criminal against the paranoiac,
    for sport
    for power

and if anyone revealed
the *Danse Macabre*
and its participants,
who would believe them?

Patient exhibited
    paranoid delusions.
Patient presented
    self-inflicted wounds.

How many decades
did the mad minister the mad?
how many post-partum melancholic
wives were sent here and abandoned?
    how many incorrigible inverts
        lobotomized?
how many "nervous breakdowns"
broken with electric shock?
Only the nearby graveyard
with its tiny, numbered stones
could give a count.

And how did it pass
that the Night Doctor
came to be known
in all the surrounding
countryside

<323>

as "Doctor Jones?"
His black Ford Cabriolet
with its yellow round lamps
prowled the back roads.
Sometimes he followed
the school buses, marked
where all the small boys lived.
He had a list
and he made house calls.

Why did my mother say:
He drives out of Torrance,
and that's where he takes you.
To the crazy house.
And he puts you in a room.
And he ties you down.
And he opens the leather bag
and there's a box inside,
   a box lined in red

And that's where he gets them,
the knives and saws.
And he'll take your legs,
and then your arms,
and you'll see it all happen,
and you'll feel everything.

And they'll keep you there,
in a room,
no arms   no legs
   in a bed
   in a room with one tiny window
and anyone could come in
and do anything to you...

<324>

2
Torrance
   is in ruins,
   has been for decades.
You walk on glass
  and broken tiles,
the walls
   graffiti-covered
   reveal the thoughts
   of marauding teens —

ARE YOU SCARED YET?
   the first one asks
Y'ALL SHOULD BE!
   says the second.

In the ruined
   lower level,
bearable by day
in slant of sunbeam —

unthinkable on
   moonless nights —

a night-dank corridor
is lined with doors
doors into tiny rooms
whose bare bricks
might once
have been padded,
a prison-slit window
at the top of each,
just large enough
to emit those screams
the thick trees muffled,
just large enough
to admit a bat
   or a spider.

<325>

What would have been
the day-room,
sunny once,
the red brick arches
and tall trees mocking
beyond the doors and windows

<326>

just as some corridors end now
in glimpses of field
   and twisted tree branch,
just as snarls of vine intrude
with the illusion
    that outside and inside
    might one day change places

or was the outside world
seen from door frame
through door frame
through outer arches

a white-eyed Moloch
whose leering face
threatened an outer world
a thousand times worse
than padded walls?

Did the attendants
and the Night Doctor
permit these vistas,
only to tell them
Go ahead and try.
Escape from Torrance,
and the whole countryside
will be on the lookout.

<327>

Search parties and guns,
rednecks and howling dogs
will track you down.

Those who left
and then came back
were never even half
of what they had been before,
their glazed eyes
    vacant
until the day
their numbered stone
was set in soil.

The words boys scrawl
on these derelict walls
do not convey their own
despair so much as what
oozes from the brickwork:

DON'T LET THEM BURN YOU!

ENTER THE BLACK HOLE!

I AM GOING TO DIE!

and perhaps the most
disturbing one,
because the truest:

FUCK MY DEAD BODY.

<328>

3
In my dreams
the brick edifice
still stands intact
in moonlight

three thousand souls
are packed inside —
none are sleeping —
six thousand eyes
and hands,
tensed and waiting —

the black Ford Cabriolet
with its gold wheel spokes
and round-eyed headlamps
pulls up in front

and the gaunt specter
of the Night Doctor
lifts something in burlap —
something still moving? —
and hoists it
over his shoulder,

fumbling for keys,
he vanishes
into a stairwell,
his private entrance
to the lower rooms —

just another boy
who disobeyed his mother,
touched himself
   in the wrong place,
reminded his stepfather
too much of his father —

<329>

who will notice
one more scream
in the chorus of screams
from those cellar windows?
Anyone hearing
just shook his head
and shuddered,
joking nervously:
Oh, that's Torrance,
the people in Torrance.
You can hear them
on summer nights.
The screaming is bad,
but the laughing,
that's worse. To be
in such a place and laugh —
now THAT'S crazy.

4

There are no ghosts at Torrance,
not in the ruined corridors,
the pain cells, the solitary
padded rooms. Perhaps the mad
already lost their ghosts here,
their ectoplasm leaking out
through the drilled skull holes,
passing with the shock current,
up and out the chimneys.
The ghosts of murderers move on,
assuredly, to crime scenes,
or to the cradles of budding
psychopaths. They fled this place.
The doctors and attendants
died in their beds, had proper wakes,
widows and heirs at the graveside,
stones with their names and dates.

<330>

No, what screams here is the ghost
of malice, and cruelty and power,
the soul of evil that says:
I am the Night Doctor.
I can do anything to anyone,
and I have found the place
in which to do it.

I'm glad we have these
little evenings together,
so glad we found
our mutual interest.
It's not easy for me
to get you out.
For chess, I tell them.
I see you've laid
the instruments in perfect order.
You could have your own practice
when they let you out of here.
No, not for a while yet.

Everything is ready.
Would you like to see
what I've got in this sack?

<331>

The Outcast

The boy is not like
   the others.
Their bikes ascend the hill,
storm down like whirlwinds.
He always walks, their wheels
   a dervish dance
      whose physics baffle him.
He passes the practice field,
hopes no one will notice him
as he carries his books
on the way to the library
(they don't wear glasses,
   don't read anything
   between June and August).
He has no idea
   what their cries mean,
   why it matters
that a ball goes
   this way
      that way.

When they let him come,
   he runs with some older boys,
over a fence he can barely scale,
   watching for dogs that bite,
to the forbidden
   apple tree.
They climb to reach
   the great red ones.

From high above
   they taunt him,
dare him to join them
at the sky-scream treetop.

<332>

He stands below.
Climbing a tree
     is one of many things
     he's not allowed to do.

They talk about baseball
     and BB guns,
the cars they'll drive
when they're old enough,
the names of girls
whose breasts have swollen.

He reaches up
     for the lower branch
     takes unripe apples,
     unmarred by bird or worm.

Walking alone,
     he sees a daytime moon,
     wonders how Earth
     might look from its craters.
He goes home to his comics,
     to the attic room
     where aliens and monsters
     plan universal mayhem.

Don't eat those apples,
     his mother warns him.
They'll give you a stomach ache.

I like them, he says.
Green apples taste better.

<333>

Rhapsodomancy

At loss for inspiration I turn
to my *Occult Encyclopedia*,
open the book at random
to see what curious lore
I might deem worthy
of a passing verse.
Maybe a curse,
a spell, an oracle or two...

The book falls open
somewhere at "R,"
I let my finger
   (the oracular one)
fly out to the left
   until it touches.
I look and read.
"Rhapsodomancy," it says,
   "Divination by means
   of opening the works
   of a poet at hazard
   and reading the verse
   which first presents itself
   oracularly."

I laugh.
So poets don't need
advice on magic.
We *are* magic.

<334>

Athena and Medusa

HE MAY BE WISE, that owl-eyed
Athena, but she's Greek
and steeped in spite. Her wrath
against Medusa just has no end.

It's not enough to have
the Gorgon's never-dying head
(thank you, brave Perseus!)
stuck to her shield,

not enough to make her watch
(she who so adores male beauty)
as handsome warriors petrify
on seeing her serpent-
    wreathed visage

not enough
that her parched lips thirst,
her black tongue
    aches for nourishment,
while wine and victuals
pass through her mouth
into a sodden heap
at neck-base

not enough that the name
    Gorgon
makes women shudder
and men avert their eyes
lest the thing they crave,
    hard upon soft,
becomes the stillness
    of rigor mortis,
an eternity of marble

<335>

not enough that mind
    should suffer:
she's shipped Medusa's body,
pure as alabaster,
no hint of monster about her

to a brothel in Smyrna
where drunken sailors,
for a few spare drachmas
pile into a dark room
to hump a headless maiden

not enough that midwives
come annually
to deliver up her monsters —
winged things with Turkish
eyebrows, egg-shell
objects that only Harpies
would dare to hatch

Oh! not enough! and all for spite,
for that day she found Poseidon,
long-limbed and sleek
entwined in the Gorgona's arms,
in the dark confines
    of Athena's temple —
buttocks and legs and bellies
spread on her very altar!

(Is there no place the gods will not go
to have their way with a woman?)
She could not punish
her father's brother-god,
but she seized Medusa,
twisted her golden, braided hair
into a gnarl of hissing serpents,
cursed her with the petrifying glare,
wild eyed, leering, black-tongued

<336>

her body goddess-fair by night,
by day a winged monstrosity,
rough skinned with
    overlapping scales,
arms ending in razor talons.

Go to some island unknown to me,
Athena cursed her,
Go hide your shame and pray I forget you.
Conceal yourself in sea caves,
or sink-hole chasms where sunlight
will not reveal you to men or gods.

For this, her wounded vanity,
five thousand years at least
Medusa pays, her debt
to Wisdom's dark side,
implacable and cruel.

<337>

The Secret Tree

I am dry. A circle of bark
peels stiffly from my crumbling limbs.
The itch of mold and termites
gives me no rest from entropy.
Leaves have not come this year.
It is rough everywhere:
parched earth has matted straw for hair
and desperate creatures huddle, homeless.
What the hot wind implies, I follow:
push out my roots to where the rains have gone,
deep, deeper, search for new rhythms
in crack and crevice, beyond the worm-world.

Dead to the wind above, bare-boned and tall,
I weave no banner poems in air, no seeds
fly out that other green may imitate:
making another like me is not the answer.
Mine is a secret growth, a sunless tree,
a new thing never seen before.
I plummet toward earth's mantle,
sprout from the roofs of caves,
make roost for the lightless chatterers,
the bats, my only friends in this sightless
and nearly soundless chasm.

<338>

Through the bottom and beyond, I grow.
Above, my seeming corpse, that monument,
betrays no life to deadly air. The dead things
around me are truly dead. I sway
in secret winds of magma, magnetic,
I drink salt waters from the hearts of geodes.
I bloom in the dark heart of everything,
that place, not Hades, but equally dreaded,
to which everything wants to, but cannot
fall. I have more branches now
than I ever could have imagined.

Squid sing to me in the ocean trenches,
plates moan tectonic as I wrap new rings
of iron and nickel around myself.
If leaf and blossom come to me now,
who shall see them? No one.
If seeds, or something like them,
issue from my branch-ends, where
will they go? Volcano-vented upward?
Or hoarded here in darkness?
The tree above seems only a dream now,
but so long as no one cuts it
and no storm dares to topple it,
I am only its bad dream. Pray
I do not awaken.

<339>

Quand Il Pleut, Il Pleut des financiers

*(Men in bowler hats descend from the clouds
in Magritte's painting, "Golconde")*

America, awake! Last night Connecticut
suffered a fall of financiers, precipitate
from aerial fleets unseen and traceable
to nowhere on or in the globe.
At dawn a gray cascade
of overcoats and bowler hats
commenced, each agent replete
with tie and unscuffed shoes,
each with a grim and businesslike

demeanor — a few, with executive
gray sideburns, clasped briefs
full of significant business plans
and letters of unlimited credit.

Only a few insomniacs
witnessed this *chute des etrangers*,
silent as dew and just as discreet,
without a flutter of parachute,
without a crease in the perfect lawns.
The anti- Newtonian host
walked with deliberate speed
to the waiting commuter trains
from whence they vanished
unnoticed into Wall Street,
courthouse and brokerage,
library and chapel, gone —
gone and never seen again!

Imposters! Who knows what plots
they hatched in their resemblance
to no one at all! Within days the banks
were belching loans; the wives at home

<340>

had well-dressed afternoon lovers;
dogs stood confused at whom to heel
or whom to bar from the kitchen door.

The birth rate rose astonishingly,
as featureless babies that refused to cry
swamped the suburban nurseries.

And this was just the start: the cloud
that made them was but a wisp
of a much larger storm, forging
its turgid thunder into an army
of Nobodies, incurable bores
intent on crowding out everyone
who's read a book or has an opinion.
Their secret handshakes and nods,
the curious little lapel pins
that your eyes can't focus on,
the sinister stripes on their ties
not corresponding to any known school
or regiment; the half-wink
they seem to use to greet one another,
smirking at others' exclusion:

these were the symptoms, alien
and alienating. There were more
like them with each passing month.
The "suits,"
as they called themselves, were here to stay.
As for the rest of us, we
were merged and acquired,
outsourced, down-sized,
shown to the door by security,
Romneyed and pension-plundered,
rezoned, foreclosed,
eminent-domained, evicted,
bankrupted and down-debited,
rust belt trailer park shantied –

<341>

just as it was planned
in their spreadsheets,
forecast in their Powerpoint
laptop PDA wireless
global master plan.

We were only here
to serve the Nobodies
on their road to acquiring
Absolutely Everything.

<342>

Sleeping With Thor

THERE MIGHT AS WELL BE a neon sign outside
that flashes "Vacancy," for all talk I get from you.
Your great blond hulk beside me, breathing,
that one arm holding me, tight as a battle trophy:
all fine and good. Dane, or Viking, or as you joked
when you dragged me back here, "The great God Thor,
in exile from Asgard," your open mouth is wordless,
as animal slumber, not quite a snore but a rumble
rolls over me. At the foot of the bed, your sandals,
somewhere safely off, that hammer named Mjolnir
that I think means more to you than boyfriends,
all fine. I should just relax and enjoy this, but for
the fact that you are sleeping with both eyes open
and I am staring into two tenantless holes where once
those commanding blue orbs had sundered my resistance.

Twice you have stirred, and wordless, twice
we have done everything you thought I wanted — god,
things I never even dreamt of! Even with all that armor on,
each touch was just at the cusp between joy and too much
to bear. If that was mead we drank, I'll toast the maker,
but will I too go eyeless into your zombie slumber?

Or are you in Asgard, where Odin even now scolds you
for your college-boy dalliance? Remember to tell him
I am a poet, and a fit companion and confidant!
Your strong hand will not release me; clad
in the tatters of what you tore from me, I must wait
for the next installment, or canto, or conquest.

Are you in and out of yourself as it conveniences?
Those blue eyes drilled me, as you enjoyed the spoils
of my all too easy surrender. But what I get
is this manikin semblance of a lover. In winning you
I find the fox's calling card, a henhouse full of carnage
and a room chill-blasted with Arctic air.

<343>

If you are but a phantom, perhaps the rest of you
will follow your errant eyes. I will wake then
embracing a suit of armor, red cape and leggings.

I'll look down empty corridors of clothes, find no one
either up your sleeves or down your trousers, the shape
of your strong legs only an imprint on the mattress.

If I reach in those vacant sockets, I'd feel my fingers touch.
I'd know the embrace that holds me was death's rigor;
I'd feel the cold hand for a pulse and find none. I'd dare
to place my lips to yours, expecting no respiration.

I think I hear a distant wind, a sigh between your ears
and mine. Perhaps it comes from Asgard, perhaps
you ride the Bifrost to return to me. Can I be bard
to your impossible beauty, if when those eyes
assume their blueness, the only words you mutter
are something about hockey practice, too much to drink,
and the need for a serious breakfast?

But there, the armored breastplate presses me still,
and there, next to our hastily thrown-off jackets,
reposes Mjolnir, the square-ended hammer of Thor.

<344>

ABOUT THE POEMS

THE BLOOD IS THE LIFE

SON OF DRACULA was originally a very short poem in the *Anniversarius* cycle of Autumn poems — a remembrance of a childhood fascination with Dracula, an adolescent nosebleed, and a brief October hospital stay in which I saw a graveyard on a nearby hillside, lit up by steel mill furnaces. A revision turned it into something more profound — a very specific memoir of childhood angst in the coal towns of Pennsylvania, and, at the end, my emergence as a poet.

A LETTER TO MUMMY is a humorous poem provoked by fellow poet Barbara A. Holland. Sometime after we had discussed a genetic peculiarity of vampires — that their children borne by nonvampire women have no bones — Barbara produced "The Consultation," a poem whose narrator demands an abortion from her doctor rather than bear a rubbery infant. My poem is a direct response to her line, "Can you imagine such a being as an adult?" I can, and here is the result. The poem is an interesting mix of humor and bitter irony. It takes the vampire myth seriously on its own terms but deals wryly with the frustrations of a boy who will never be able to join the Order of Vertebrae.

SCENES FROM A MEXICAN VAMPIRE MOVIE started as a dream, related in the first stanza. The rest of the poem happened when I awoke from the dream, rushed to the computer, and started typing. This poem was adapted, word-for-word, as a comic, in the first issue of *Midnight Graffiti*.

THE SPIDERS was a mere tidbit in my early book, *The Pumpkined Heart*, merely a nature observation about spider webs on an early morning lawn. This expansion puts spiders in context as worse-than-vampires. As my uncle Bela says, "The vampire drinks the blood. But the spider! the spider drinks ... *everything!*" My friends Pieter Vanderbeck and Robert Dodge contributed to the arachnophobia of my household with their lurid tales of New England barn spiders. John Crompton's informative book, *The Spider*, was also an inspiration.

DAWN elaborates on the problems vampires have with mirrors, and the ironies of the Goth obsession with costume. My vampire can see neither himself nor the clothes he dons. The ennui of the 300-year-old vampire is conveyed with a touch of Dorian Gray. I had never thought previously about pushing someone through a chain-link fence, and it does seem a novelty.

THINGS SEEN IN GRAVEYARDS

This cycle of poems has grown over the years, and will continue to grow. The earliest poems in this grouping were revised in 2007 for publication as a separate chapbook.

THE TURK'S MAUSOLEUM and SACRIFICE are from Mount Auburn in Cambridge.

In NIGHT WALKER, I witnessed an elderly lady sleepwalking, and only found out two days later that she had walked into the nearby river and drowned. In the same cemetery (West Newton, Pennsylvania) I saw a late night grave robbery, recounted in NIGHT SHIFT.

<345>

TRYSTING PLACE refers to the delicious pioneer graveyard in Edinboro, Pennsylvania, where old graves moldered along the edge of a glacial lake. Untold numbers of college students lost their innocence on those soft lawns.

MIDSUMMER NIGHT is from the same place, a nearby grove of trees filled with bats and fireflies.

WEST POINT is from the mass grave of cadets who were sent off to fight in the Mexican War, and is also a nod to Walt Whitman.

JUDGE HATHORNE'S GRAVE, AT SALEM is based on seeing a tree whose roots were wrapped around a gravestone in Salem, Massachusetts.

THE FORGOTTEN GRAVESTONE and THE SWAN POINT GHOUL are both from Providence, Rhode Island.

A newspaper account of a prison work detail sent to an island burial ground in New York harbor prompted the poem, HART ISLAND. It is not a fantasy.

AFTER THE STORM takes us back to Edinboro, Pennsylvania where, in a more modern graveyard, I heard an unearthly wailing. The ideas for this poem come from studies of Iroquois lore. Among their beliefs was the charming notion that chopping down a tree over old bones would bring dead animals back to life.

Back in Mount Auburn, I found crows all over Longfellow's sarcophagus, and remembered the mutual dislike he and Poe expressed, in THE ARGUMENT.

New England vampire lore is thin, but the Exeter, Rhode Island case of 1799 has poignant details. The idea of dead family members coming back for brothers and sisters is common to many cultures, and is probably based on an attempt to explain why many members of the same family died one after another. Before Pasteur's conception of bacteria as a cause of disease, such cases seemed to be God's work, or the Devil's. AN EXETER VAMPIRE, 1799, is written mostly in lines of nine syllables. I felt, somehow, that this clipped line evoked the feeling of passivity among the Tillinghast children.

When I speculated publicly about a possible Lovecraft-cult connection to a Rhode Island grave desecration, a Pawtucket police detective invited me to the scene of the crime. This is related in MRS. WEEDEN, OF PAWTUCKET.

THE EXHUMATION OF GOETHE is based on a detailed newspaper account of the "maceration" of Goethe's skeleton by the East German government, in an attempt to turn the great poet's remains into a tourist attraction, like the mummy in Lenin's tomb. Most of the details here are factual.

I started THE HARVESTMAN several years before it finally spun its web to completion. It's a very formal poem, taking its form from Grey's "Elegy in a Country Churchyard."

ACELDEMA, THE FIELD OF BLOOD is a legendary cemetery in Israel, a place where only strangers are buried.

MINERS' CEMETERY IN ATACAMA, CHILE must be the loneliest cemetery on earth, and the driest.

MY LIFE AS AN INCUBUS

WATER SPRITE was inspired by a midnight bicycle ride along the Seekonk River in Providence, and the appearance — and disappearance — of a nude figure alongside a lagoon.

MY LIFE AS AN INCUBUS is an expansion of a shorter poem, a fantasy

<346>

about becoming a gender-shifting incubus/succubus. After a rereading of Marlowe's *Doctor Faustus*, I added the opening section detailing my bargain with Mephistopheles.

THE WAKING DREAM was written just after the premonition of the death of a loved one. The vision turned out to be false, but the dream was an intense one: a disembodied spirit, waking me from a sound sleep, all but crying out: "Remember me! Remember me! What did I look like? What did I mean to you? Quickly, quickly, or I am lost!" Then, the sense of the Loved One's spirit dissipating, becoming nothing.

A HAUNTING is a related poem, about memories that come fleetingly before sleep.

★★★

FÊTE. Of all my poems, *Fête* might be my own favorite, and the one which involved the most subtle process of creation and construction. The poem culminated a long, hopeless, and unfruitful infatuation, and was a winter night's catharsis of revenge, rejection — a stab against the futility of thwarted affections.

The following paragraphs are what I had to say about this poem in 1985:

The poem came unplanned after three nights of penetrating dreams. Giant bats, the giant owl sentinels, the country churchyard, the vestments of the sorcerer, all came to me as colorful *images*, but not as words. The dreams were visions in which the Loved One was mysteriously abducted and brought into my power for an act of revenge.

On the fourth night, I doused all the house lights, placed a candle and some pens and papers atop a small organ console in my living room, put on the Berlioz *Symphonie Fantastique* on the stereo, and began writing. The first 65 lines came in one loop — writing a few lines, reading them aloud, then writing again. Then, the incantation stanzas (italics in the text) came to me, willing the Loved One's kidnapping — then all the lines before the final stanza came in one unbroken stream in about forty-five minutes.

The Berlioz symphony played through a second time as I looked at what I had written and tried to decide what came next — would the poem continue in some way or would there be an abrupt end? How would the sorcerer kill, punish or transform the Loved One?

The ending of the poem — lines that spilled onto the page without plan — was to be exactly the opposite of my conscious intention. The sorcerer has conquered the Loved One with magic, is prepared to enact the most horrible revenge — and then his will collapses and the expected murder ritual becomes a *wedding!*

What astonished me, and careful readers of the poem as well, is how the entire poem is littered with symbols that are the trappings of a wedding turned inside out: the red carpet of leaves, stars as witnesses, the church, the Pleiades (Seven Sisters) as bridesmaids as well as a longstanding symbol of hymeneal summer, the bats as doves, the arbor of batwings, the owls as the disapproving parents, the elopement through the window by bat abduction, the cat as bribed duenna, and, finally, the rings. My unconscious set a trap and I literally wrote myself into it.

With the exception of some pronoun changes and the removal of several redundant words, the poem stands exactly as written in first draft. It passed like a whirlwind through my consciousness. *Craft* can take credit for only so much;

<347>

reason for so much — but there is still a magic, mad element in some poems in which we must let the unconscious literally be our guide. Whether the unconscious is a computer comprising all the poems we have read before, or whether it possesses some mythic core, we will probably never know, but the effect is the same.

In a more direct way, *Fête* was a response to a challenge in the immediate poetry circle around me. I had been impressed with Barbara Holland's "Black Sabbat" and "Not Now, Wanderer," poems of elemental magic ritual, sorcery, and obsessive love. Had I not read them, I would probably not have cast my *Fête* into this vein. The *language* of the poem — a little Poe and a stark-mad Shelley — come from my own absorption in their language, of course. It is the *combination* of the plot, the language, and the dual-level images, however, that makes this poem so startling even to its author. I consider its creation a case study in the poetic craft — the real reason why I devote so many words to it in notes.

So much for 1985. I did not touch this poem again until 1997, when I began to prepare the present volume, I finally summoned the courage to revise it. I have added some new lines here and there, and revised others, purely for the sake of making the narrative more clear. In other cases I found that I had spontaneously written many whole stanzas in blank verse, with only a few jarring short or long lines. It was simple enough to make these lines more metrical.

Other passages, especially the incantation, I tended to leave alone. Years of reading them aloud to audiences convinced me that they worked. All these years later, this poem still thrills and frightens me.

★ ★ ★

EDGAR AND HELEN recounts, with not too many liberties, some of the essence of the doomed romance between Edgar Allan Poe and the Providence poet Sarah Helen Whitman. I had fun playing with the flowery speech of suitors, and with Helen's various objections to the proposed marriage. The sad thing is that she did love Poe, but her family opposed the match. It was Poe himself, however, with drinking and a laudanum overdose episode, who caused the engagement to be called off just as it was about to become official.

At the end, I have Poe in misery, inflicting imaginary tortures on his tormentors, and then heading south to a "darker mistress," his own death the next year. Do not take this poem as literal account of the affair: I have hidden secrets of my own in this poem. I have said much more about Poe and Helen in my book, *Last Flowers: The Romance Poems of Edgar Allan Poe and Sarah Helen Whitman.*

THE PORTRAIT OF DORIAN GRAY appeared in a shortened version in the first edition of this book, and then I suppressed it. I had not managed to express what I wanted to say, and finally I think I have arrived at my own twist on the theme of the immortal beauty and the price he pays for his immutable state. And in case you're wondering, no, it's not about anyone I know.

LUCY, A VERSE MYSTERY is a short story in blank verse. It features actual historical and literary personages: Edgar Allan Poe, his Providence fiancee Sarah Helen Whitman and her family, and Mrs. Whitman's curious friend, the poet William Pabodie. This poem extrapolates from family secrets on Benefit Street, and connects Poe's "The Raven" to a verse by Walter Scott.

<348>

THE CREEPERS

THE MESSENGERS specifically evokes the image of newspaper pages blowing aimlessly in the street around the Atlantic Avenue subway station in Brooklyn — one of the most forlorn, depressing and Godforsaken public places in the transit system. One night the newspapers were shuffling about even though there was no wind at all.

THE CREEPERS, previously titled "Halloween Night," is a Manhattan poem, detailing the images and thoughts on a cab ride and walk home to 95th Street from a Halloween party thrown by poet Shirley Powell. Going north from Abingdon Square along the far West Side of Tenth Avenue, one saw derelict buildings and derelict people, some perhaps not even people at all but merely animated heaps of rotting clothing. By the time I got home, I was wary of everything: the alley cats, the garbage cans, even the ivy clinging to the brownstone. Think of this as an impressionistic night piece, a nocturne of New York's ever-amazing landscape.

NIGHTERS is a wickedly perverse look at the riders on the last possible train home from Manhattan to Brooklyn on a Sunday morning before dawn. During my years of residence in Brooklyn I would sometimes ride this debauchee's express, or, as I jokingly called it, "The Vampire Special." The poem is fun to read aloud, adding a certain Lugosi touch toward the final lines. This poem premiered at Emilie Glen's Manhattan poetry salon where it never failed to produce groans, shivers, and a nervous fingering of rosaries.

HE'S GOING TO KILL ME TONIGHT is based on a story related to me by my late friend Jerome Bona, about an obsessive neighbor lady who slid paranoid notes under people's doors.

THE COLLECTORS represents another passion I shared in common with poet Barbara A. Holland — an admiration for the strange universe of Belgian Surrealist painter Rene Magritte. Unlike the hard Surrealists who favor distorted planes and unrecognizable landscapes, Magritte achieves his magic by employing a realistic or even photographic representation of a plausible world, mixing the familiar with some mysterious or even physically impossible elements. "The Collectors" is an amalgam of several Magritte paintings: one shows a variety of household objects (and a lion) neatly placed along the edges of a winding road. Another is a seascape in which little Belgian townhouses have been stacked up helter-skelter like a child's blocks. This is the magic of Magritte — taking a mundane beach or urban perspective and making it utterly mysterious. One cannot help but look at the stack of displaced houses and ask — by whom was this all done, and for what purpose?

CHAIN SMOKER is a ghost poem on one level and a protest against the pollution of one's personal breathing space on a second level. Nonsmokers have grown quite attached to this poem; the human chimneys sometimes leave the room when I read it. For the record, I smoked a pipe in my college days, and gave it up for three reasons: (1) I set two coats on fire by absent-mindedly tucking away my Calabash in a pocket; (2) I discovered that food actually has a taste if you permit your taste buds to live, and (3) I saw what one drop of pure nicotine does to a laboratory rat — annihilation within seconds. The idea of carrying a miniature, personal Dachau in one's mouth is not pleasant.

<349>

THE SORCERER'S COMPLAINT is the beginning of an ongoing colloquy between myself and fellow New York poet Barbara A. Holland. The many readings we frequented together were enlivened by a series of challenge-and-response poems. When Barbara and I had a long dinner during which I joked about installing a multi-tentacled Lovecraftian creature to protect the Poet's Press Chelsea loft from burglars, she went home and wrote "Take Flight to Montreal." This poem is my reply, adding reference to the uncanny fact that her regular delivery of copy for our joint magazine, *Poets Fortnightly*, was inevitably accompanied by a downpour of rain. This "personal drizzle" on her raccoon coat made her entrance like that of a very aristocratic, but very soggy, mouse.

UNWELCOME COMPANY. Have you ever been awakened at two in the morning by inexplicable cries, close at first and then fading rapidly? This poem recounts such a nocturnal visitation during my abode in Brooklyn. What I took for Banshees, the Irish death-omen-bearers, turned out to be twelve Puerto Rican boys on bicycles, setting off their toy *Star Trek* communicators in unison as they sped by. So much for Celtic mythology!

THE DEAD END is based on a dream — a not uncommon dream of being among those who are dead, in a strange zone where they have taken up residence.

CURSES! recounts an actual experiment in the efficacy of Egyptian magic. One All Saint's Eve I invoked *Ammit,* the Eater of the Dead, from Egyptian mythology, with the help of a few fellow employees, as a symbolic curse against an oppressive and monomaniacal employer.

We were joking, as I do not believe in magic, but I led my guests to take it as a serious ceremony. We put his photograph inside a magic circle, in which were written various names and attributes of The Eater of the Dead. At an appropriate moment, the photograph was set on fire — but his eye refused to burn!

The intended victim is still alive and kicking, so I'm afraid that Ammit, part crocodile, part hippopotamus, part lion, missed dinner that night. Still, some curses are slow in working, and crocodiles are rather slow in making that transatlantic crossing. It is even possible that Ammit has a waiting list! (I also have a delicious fantasy that every alligator in Florida has his picture pinned to the inside of its hat.) I await the obituary.

THE GRIM REAPER is based on an old German folksong which was set as a choral piece by Brahms.

In 1998, I read about THE EAR MOUND IN KYOTO, and a ceremony commemorating the 400th anniversary of the burial of the ears from 100,000 slain or mutilated Koreans. The poem is fanciful in detail but accurate in history. The ears were taken, and the warlord Toyotomi Hideyoshi (actually a great hero of feudal Japan) did die suddenly just a year after the ears were brought to him as trophies. Japan still refuses to return the ears; hence this poem.

THE NEW TENANT documents my recent move to a building infested with art students.

THE BLACK HUNTSMAN is my adaptation of a Victor Hugo poem, which I updated to include war criminal Dick Cheney.

<350>

DIE LAUGHING

VALKYRIES ON ROUTE 128 came to me after watching too many hours of Wagner operas on Public Television.

For THE McWILLIAMS' COFFEE TABLE, I owe a debt to Shirley Powell, who wrote of the theft of country gravestones for coffee tables.

While reading over some piano music by Robert Schumann, I came across a piano piece about KNECHT RUPRECHT, the dark companion of Santa Claus who punished bad children. I invented all the imagery surrounding him, trying for a Brothers Grimm atmosphere. The piece turned out to be a very effective actor's monologue. Imagine it read by the late, great Boris Karloff.

CHRISTMAS VERSES are doggerel, written to amuse my friends.

THE ANACONDA POEMS was inspired by reading, in the Science Section of *The New York Times*, about the sex life of the giant anaconda, the world's largest snake.

GORGON AT THE WEDDING (originally titled "On the Greek Side") reflects my fascination with some of the minor figures of Greek mythology. The Greek monsters tend to come in threes. Perseus killed Medusa, even though other mortals who saw her turned to stone, by the device of only looking at her reflection in his highly polished shield as he lopped off her head. Two other Gorgons survived, however — Medusa's sisters Euryale and Stheno. One of them even wrote a dirge for Medusa that was played by flutists at the Olympic games.

THE SAILOR AND THE OAK NYMPHS is based on Greek mythology related to the sacred oak and Rhea. This poem is from my *Anniversarius* cycle.

END OF THE WORLD, another autumn *Anniversarius* poem, is just a fantasy about people — instead of leaves — turning colors and blowing away.

SQUANTO'S WIND. The John Hancock Building in Boston had to be surrounded with covered sidewalks for several years because window panes kept popping from their casements, hurtling to the pavement below. I imagined this as the doings of an enraged *manitou*. My early version of the poem described only the window problem. It turns out the entire construction was jinxed, so now I have added more details.

A shorter version of AUTUMN ON MARS was written several years back and counted as part of the ongoing *Anniversarius* series. I made it longer and elaborated on the anatomy of the imaginary Martians, with a wave of the tentacle to Ray Bradbury (whose Martians were admittedly far more humanoid). But no one can say "Mars" and "Halloween" in the same breath without evoking the Master of *The Martian Chronicles*.

DIAGNOSIS OF E. A. POE is my reaction to a silly newspaper story in which a medical researcher claimed to have "solved" the mystery of Poe's 1849 death in Baltimore. In this theory, a case of rabies would account for Poe's symptoms as he lay in a Baltimore hospital. We'll stick with the traditional death by alcohol, but the rabies idea led me to this poem.

HERE AT THE POINT is for inquiring minds. The people who run Swan Point Cemetery, a fine and noble establishment, have some strange foibles, one of which is their mounting obsession about preventing photography of the splendid monuments and landscape of their garden cemetery. Since this conflicts with our annual Lovecraft ceremonies in Swan Point — very public events indeed — I sent a secret agent to attend the security meeting that preceded the bizarre installation

<351>

of floodlights at Lovecraft's grave one recent Halloween.

A NIGHT IN EDDIE'S APARTMENT is from Summer 2004, and recounts surrealistic impressions of a stay in Paterson, New Jersey. I thank Eddie Rivera for his hospitality, and for his permission to publish this intimate glimpse into the home life of one of New Jersey's most outrageous poets. Note: all stuffed animals in this poem were over the age of eighteen.

WEST OF ARKHAM

AT LOVECRAFT'S GRAVE was one of the best fruits of my first sojourn in Providence (1985-1993). This memorial tribute to America's greatest horror writer is now publicly read at Lovecraft's grave at least twice yearly, to my great delight. It was the basis of a limited edition chapbook of the same title, and was reprinted during the official Lovecraft Centennial, and appears also as an appendix to my play, *Night Gaunts*. I'm afraid the poem won't mean much to those unfamiliar with HPL. Persons named in the poem include the eminent Lovecraft scholar and biographer, S.T. Joshi, and Carl Johnson, the actor who would later play Lovecraft in my play. The day of this poem marked my first meetings with the latter-day "Lovecraft gang." I've been honored that this poem has been read by Mr. Johnson and others at more than two decades' worth of annual HPL ceremonies at Swan Point.

MAKER OF MONSTERS, MAKER OF GODS was a birthday poem for eminent American horror writer Frank Belknap Long. I met Frank Long when I was asked to conduct a television interview with him about his mentor, H.P. Lovecraft. We became friends — I only regret meeting him so close to his decline and demise. We had been neighbors in Chelsea almost two decades earlier, but had never met.

HEARING THE WENDIGO is about the legendary wind elemental supposedly known to all the American Indians from the Great Plains to Hudson Bay. Ever since Algernon Blackwood wrote about the Wendigo in his short story set in the Canadian woods, it has become the stuff of campfire stories and late-night ghost sessions, almost endlessly embellished upon. Everyone who tells a Wendigo story adds something to it.

DREAMING OF UR-R'LYEH has strange origins. I was invited by Peter Lamborn Wilson to contribute to an "Astral Convention" in Antarctica. The premise was that all the participants would think or dream about Antarctica simultaneously, and submit whatever they wrote as a result for publication. The resulting book should, alone, be convincing evidence that there is presently no telepathic power in the human psyche. People saw and envisioned exactly what they were inclined to see, principally sex, drugs and anarchy. My own "waking dream" was influenced by Poe and Lovecraft, specifically Lovecraft's Antarctic novel, *At the Mountains of Madness*. I had also read a book about Shackleton's Antarctic expedition, from which I obtained the descriptions I used of solar and atmospheric conditions. There are many things about this poem, considerably expanded since its first publication, that I still can't explain. I won't try.

WITH POE ON MORTON STREET PIER is from the *Anniversarius* cycle. It's one of my most-revised poems. It began as a simple, lonely description of sunset on the piers in Greenwich Village, but over the years, as I learned more

<352>

about Poe's comings and goings, I realized I had written the poem on the spot where Poe first disembarked in New York.

THE HERMIT'S HOUSE is a poetic response to a quaint drawing by Scott Kerr, the illustrator of my anthology, *May Eve*. The following poem, WEST OF ARKHAM, is in a similar vein. The opening line echoes the beginning of Lovecraft's tale, "The Colour Out of Space."

LOW TIDE is based, as its epigraph indicates, on a dream recorded in Lovecraft's journals. Lovecraft's childhood homes were all a short walking distnace from the Seekonk River.

FRANK AND LYDA is a highly condensed account of my strange friendship with Frank Belknap Long and his tormented wife, Lyda Arco Long. Although Frank and I had splendid conversations, and I came to appreciate his poetry and the gentle spirit of his short stories, everything was overshadowed by his wife's advanced mental illness. A sad ending for a fine writer.

SNOFRU THE MAD was based on reading about the Pharaoh's life and times in Gardiner's *History of Ancient Egypt*. Footnotes:

(1) Snofru or Snefru was Pharaoh in the Fourth Dynasty and the immediate predecessor of Khufu (Cheops), builder of the Great Pyramid. Historians are baffled as to why Snofru built himself four separate pyramids.

(2) Snofru was the first Pharaoh to enclose his name in a cartouche.

When Gardiner noted the "unpalatable" thought that Snofru had built four pyramids, the whole idea of this poem sprang forth in my mind, completely formed. The historical details in the poem are correct, but I have invented the mad Pharaoh's reasoning.

POEM FOUND ON THE NECK OF A DEER, KILLED IN THE BLACK FOREST, GERMANY, 1975 (originally titled REUNION) is my contribution to werewolf lore. It is much expanded from the version in this book's first edition, with a substantial plot change. In the early edition, my protagonist was the host and the werewolf the guest. It didn't read well, and making the werewolf the host also allowed me to add the Baroness werewolf as well.

Beware! IN THE GHOUL-HAUNTED WOODLAND is only for those willing to tolerate some juvenilia for the same of a few terrifying lines. I had discarded this poem many years ago, but lines of it came back to me during a long bout with migraine headaches — as a persistent refrain, as it were. A few lines near the end seem to be irretrievably lost. I did "touch up" some of the opening stanzas a little, but I fear I can never recreate the naive quality of the original. It was written in when I was in tenth grade, smitten with Poe, graveyards and the morbid vision of following the bier of a loved one into the grove of enchanted cypresses. Even then, I already knew that something evil, alien and *hungry* was waiting in the branches. If you read this poem aloud, and act out the final stanza, I think you will see why I kept it.

A LITERARY REVIVAL is a poem from the dystopian world of Ray Bradbury's novel *Fahrenheit 451*. In this horrifying future, firemen are part of a secret police network, bursting into people's homes in order to *burn* books. Books are forbidden and to own a private library is a state crime.

The specific impetus for this poem was a late night glimpse of the malevolent geometries of New York's Cooper Square, in which I suddenly saw an imagined scene that belonged in the world of *Fahrenheit 451*: rows of bedraggled derelicts

<353>

standing in a long line waiting for books, not to be read but to be used as *fuel*. What if one man in that line were a criminal, a booklover? What if he had to burn the books as he read them, or freeze to death? A ghastly vision.

It had not occurred to me at the time of writing, but the poem has another level of aptness: Cooper Square is at the south end of that stretch of Fourth Avenue that was once Book Row. The glorious old booksellers with their dusty, perilously perched balconies and mysterious cellars are nearly all gone now. How we miss them!

WHEN WORLDS COLLIDE was provoked by hearing a poet of religious bent trotting out the old "argument by design" to prove the existence of god. Such a perfect universe as ours, so the argument goes, could only be created by God. I had just recently seen the NASA photographs of distant, colliding galaxies, and I mentioned this as my rebuttal, saying, "If you lived in one of those galaxies, you wouldn't believe nature was designed by God." For days after this conversation, I continued to think about the NASA photos, which I had seen in *The New York Times*. Then I began to dream about them, and this poem rapidly came to pass. The line "alu marana echtho karani," translated at the end of the poem, is in an imaginary language from one of the distant planets. The poem's title, of course, refers to Philip Wylie's famous screenplay and novel.

THE TREE AT LOVECRAFT'S GRAVE returns to the same locale as the earlier poem AT LOVECRAFT'S GRAVE. This time the lordly spreading beech tree is the center of attention. This poem has now joined the small collection of ceremonial pieces performed occasionally at HPL's grave. It has taken on a special poignancy since the destruction of the tree in a storm several years ago.

KEZIAH MASON and KEZIAH'S GEOMETRY LESSONS are imagined biographies of the witch from H.P. Lovecraft's "Dreams in the Witch House," and of Brown Jenkin, her familiar. Brown Jenkin, with his rat's body and a human face, is one of the most unsettling creatures in all of Lovecraft's tales.

THE MIND, THE EYE, THE TENTACLE is another "occasional" poem, but it far transcends the assignment of creating something "Lovecraftian" for a gravesite reading. This one is pretty much for HPL specialists, since it includes three monstrous beings invented by The Old Gent, but I encourage others to read it — it's actually a serious philosophical poem.

MIDNIGHT ON BENEFIT STREET, 1935 attempts to create the mixture of splendor and squalor that Lovecraft knew in his home town in the 1930s. I included all the landmarks one would see (then and now) in a midnight walk along Benefit Street, with a few nods to Poe. This is a poem I enjoy, but I recognize that it will be of far less resonance for those who don't live in our haunted city of Providence.

UNDER LOVECRAFT'S GRAVE is a darkly comic play for four voices, written to be performed at H.P. Lovecraft's grave in Swan Point Cemetery. It can also be performed on-stage with actors standing inside coffins.

<354>

SECRETS OF LIFE AND DEATH

Thrills and chills in HUNCHBACK ASSISTANT TELLS ALL. Despite all my years of watching horror films, I had never written a Frankenstein poem. This long cycle of poems, which will almost certainly have a sequel, comes entirely from the world of the great Universal horror films of the 1930s and 1940s.

Mary Shelley never gave Dr. Frankenstein a hunchback assistant, so I let Fritz the hunchback set the record straight. And since we are in the tabloid era, this is a hunchback whose sex life (real or imagined) has quite a few surprises in store for the unwary reader.

The creation scenes, involving not only electricity but an animating elixir, will strike a chord for those who have read Lovecraft's tale, "Herbert West, Reanimator."

The hunchback's proclamations during the storm scene indicate he has absorbed not only Mary Shelley, but a little of her friend Lord Byron as well.

The reference to Werther in the poem is to Goethe's *The Sorrows of Young Werther*, a book which provoked a number of adolescent suicides.

***

NIGHTS AT THE STRAND was the result of visiting Scottdale, Pennsylvania, the town of my birth, where I was given a guided tour of The Geyer Performing Arts Center, in the restored movie theater where, as a child, I saw all the monster movies that warped me forever. This is my love letter to the old movie house. I can still recite, pretty much in order, all the titles of all the Saturday double-features I saw there.

SOMETHING THERE IS IN THE ATTIC lingered in my portfolio for decades as an unfinished sketch. In 2011, in a fury of revisions, I was finally able to unfold this into the fantasy it was meant to be. It might be one of the poems to be quoted someday on my obelisk.

SINCE THE OLD ONES CAME BACK TO EARTH is what might be termed a "tentacle sex" poem. Lovecraft never went beyond suggestion of what it is the creatures from other dimensions might want with us. The idea that soft flesh is a sufficient inducement for Elder God invasion is unsettling, but here it is. This was written for one of the Lovecraft birthday commemorations at Swan Point Cemetery.

WHIPPOORWILL ROAD

In MIDNIGHT WATER, I remember childhood summers in the woods of Pennsylvania.

MILKWEED SEEDS started out as a little, wispy, nature poem. A trifle, which I have now turned into a new mythology.

WHOM NONE BUT THE SHATTERED STONES RECALL was published in a shorter, more imprecise version in *The Pumpkined Heart*. The poem specifically laments the filling-in of the swamps and the construction of campus buildings on a huge stretch of beautiful marshland behind Edinboro State College in Pennsylvania. In the earlier poem I had merely *suggested* that some enormous subterranean being dwelled beneath these waters. This version is far more emphatic, and specifically identifies the nonhuman dweller as the power behind the

<355>

famed Iroquois founding father and the sorcerer Atotarho. As for the appearance of the lake and swamp dweller, I can only ask the reader to conjecture. The name Atotarho, however, means "The Entangled One."

GHOSTS is just a passing thought, but an intriguing one. What if there *are* ghosts, and if they exist only because there's nowhere else for them to go?

WHIPPOORWILL ROAD takes its central theme — the snatching of the souls of the dying by whippoorwills — from tales of H.P. Lovecraft, who asserted that the degenerate locals around his mythical Arkham believed the birds capable of such nastiness. In my childhood, whose summers were largely spent at a grandparents' house surrounded by Appalachian woods, the whippoorwills were an invisible, but omnipresent part of the night world. This poem was written a while back on a train ride to Boston, but was revised in order to include the sounds of the whippoorwills themselves. I have tinkered with this poem more than almost any other I have written. I hope this latest version is the most lucid. It was not always clear to readers just what was going on here.

THE SKEPTIC is a Lovecraftian tingler intended to frighten one who professed complete indifference to the supernatural. It invokes a dream-dweller, stirring to life and creating nightmares—even for the most hardened disbeliever.

The lyric poem, BY MOONLIGHT, SURELY, THEY'LL DANCE was written in my college town, Edinboro, Pennsylvania, at the lakeside graves of the town's first settlers. The graves, from the late 1790s, were quite literally exposed to the elements thanks to the erosion of the hillside at the lake edge. A necrophilic art student even extracted bone fragments from the wild, grape-infested spot. The old cemetery was a favorite trysting place for the more audacious students in the 1960s — a great elm- and maple-lined graveyard with quaint tombstones, often laced with mist from the quiet lake. That the cemetery on summer nights hosted so many death-defying undergraduate undulations could only have a stimulating effect upon the pioneers below. I have repunctuated this early poem more in keeping with my present style, but much of it is actually a long run-on, taken in large Whitmanesque breaths.

MAY EVE is a Lovecraftian monologue, pure and simple. It is intended to be read aloud. The reader begins calmly, but by the final lines, he is stark, raving mad. This is a very effective piece at readings, and a natural for Thespians.

TODESBLUMEN is a tale often repeated by my maternal grandmother as her own actual experience at the death of an aunt. I have changed her into a little boy merely to avoid the problems of too many feminine pronouns. The rose blooming in winter and the specter of Death tapping on the window three times were traditions accepted in the family, who emigrated from Alsace. They had a German name (Diebold) and spoke German, so I took the liberty of inventing the German term "Todesblumen." My thanks to Annette Hayn for correcting my original title, which was "Blumenstod."

AN EXPECTATION OF PRESENCES is another of my graveyard soliloquies, but it is more. Here I posit my theory of immortality. Ghosts are the *only* survivors. People who believe in God and Heaven are utterly and completely dead, having surrendered their ego and will. So spit in the eye of the priest — refuse Supreme Unction. Face the universe alone and you will have a fighting chance of becoming a ghost.

<356>

SINKHOLES was provoked by a colloquium talk given by Prof. Jean Walton at University of Rhode Island, in which the topography of her native Vancouver was described. I think certain people need to be made to worry that the earth might open up and swallow them.

DOCTOR JONES & OTHER TERRORS

It is difficult to speak about DOCTOR JONES. It took me a lifetime to write it without getting the shakes. I will never know how much of it is true, but to the small child inside me, it is all true. You be the judge.

TORRANCE merges the very real horror of a 3,000-patient Pennsylvania mental hospital into which the state dumped psychotic killers to mingle with the general population of patients. When I discovered, on-line, a set of photographs of the ruins of this psychological snake-pit, I connected it to the "Doctor Jones" legend. When I was a child, a trip to Torrance was understood to be a one-way ticket.

THE OUTCAST is really about the type of boy who grows up to be, well, someone like me. Monsters and comics have their uses.

RHAPSODOMANCY is about the marvel of coincidence. A poet's life is full of such moments, so much so that they become expected.

ATHENA AND MEDUSA explains how three beautiful Greek sisters became the terrifying Gorgons, and offers some counsel on dealing with Athena.

THE SECRET TREE is another poem that floated around in manuscript for decades. The sinister nature of the speaking voice eluded me.

QUAND IL PLEUT, IL PLEUT DES FINANCIERS is another very old poem, inspired by several of Magritte's canvasses depicting identical men in bowler hats descending upon a city street.

SLEEPING WITH THOR was an unfinished sketch about waking up with an inert bedfellow. Only after seeing the wonderful film *Thor* did I realize who I had spent the night with.

<357>

IMAGES AND ILLUSTRATIONS

Most of the images used in this book are digital art by the author, made from original digital photos and from Public Domain sources.

Dancing skeletons on inside title page by Albrecht Durer. Frontispiece from First Edition of Oscar Wilde's *The Portrait of Dorian Gray*, by Henry Keen.

"Lucy, A Verse Mystery." Engraving of Providence in 1844; photos of St. John's Churchyard and Mrs. Whitman's house by the author.

Photo montage of John Hancock Building and Squanto by the author.

Photo and digital art for "The Tree At Lovecraft's Grave" by the author.

Photo of Strand Theater/Geyer Performing Arts Center by the author.

"Doctor Jones" and "Torrance" digital art by the author, from the chapbook *Doctor Jones and Other Terrors*.

Colliding Galaxies from NASA via the Hubble Telescope.

"The Harvestman," digital art by the author, based on an image from Wikimedia Commons.

"Aceldema" Map from George Sandys *Relation of a Journey begun Anno Domini 1610*, second edition, 1621.

"Fête" and "By Moonlight, Surely, They'll Dance." Pen-and-ink drawings by Scott Kerr, from the 1975 limited edition chapbook of the poem, and from *May Eve: A Festival of Supernatural Poetry* (1975).

The cover art is a painting by Caspar David Friedrich, *The Abbey in the Oak Wood* (1809-1810).

<358>

ABOUT THIS BOOK

The body type for this book consists of several variants of Aldine, designed by Hermann Zapf to complement his earlier type family Palatino. Aldine is named after Aldus Manutius, the great Renaissance printer and book publisher, who based his font designs on letterforms from Roman stone carvings.

The title-page is set in Galliard, a French Oldstyle type introduced in 1978 and based on type designs by Robert Granjon in the 16th Century. The type was designed by Mike Parker of Mergenthaler.

The arabesque title-page border is by Alessandro Paganini, an early Venetian printer. Paganini's block initials, with a newly-designed letter "W," are used throughout the book. The Paganini design elements have been used in all five editions of this book.

<359>

www.ingramcontent.com/pod-product-compliance
Lightning Source LLC
Chambersburg PA
CBHW031603110426
42742CB00037B/819